Best Movie Scenes

*549 Memorable Bank
Robberies, Car Chases, Duels,
Haircuts, Job Interviews,
Swearing Scenes, Window
Scenes and Others, by Topic*

Second Edition

SANFORD LEVINE

McFarland & Company, Inc., Publishers
Jefferson, North Carolina, and London

ISBN 978-0-7864-7091-4
softcover : acid free paper ∞

LIBRARY OF CONGRESS CATALOGUING DATA ARE AVAILABLE

BRITISH LIBRARY CATALOGUING DATA ARE AVAILABLE

Front cover image: *from left* Tim Holt, Humphrey Bogart, Walter Huston
in *The Treasure of the Sierra Madre,* 1948 (Warner Bros./Photofest)

Manufactured in the United States of America

*McFarland & Company, Inc., Publishers
Box 611, Jefferson, North Carolina 28640
www.mcfarlandpub.com*

For anyone who has ever felt
that a particular movie scene was
made just to make them happy

Table of Contents

Introduction   1

Introduction

Movie nuts don't wear dog tags to identify themselves but I can usually spot one when I see one. That's because they still go to the movies for a particular favorite scene and can be recognized as the only members of the audience who leave when the scene is over, usually before the movie is finished. This is precisely what happened the afternoon I snuck off to the Thalia, a revival house in the Upper West Side of Manhattan, to see *Grand Illusion* for the fifteenth time. A remorseful Erich von Stroheim was just explaining to the gravely wounded Pierre Fresnay that he had been aiming for his leg when I spotted Arnold Zellermeyer in the audience. As a member of the Best Neck Brace Scenes Fan Club, he had more right to be there than I. The dying Fresnay was telling von Stroheim, "At 150 yards it was a difficult shot." When the scene was over Zellermeyer and I found ourselves the only ones leaving the theater. I caught up with him in the lobby, where we both agreed that movies like this were made just to make us happy. Though it had been nearly 17 years since I had last seen him, he hadn't changed much. A bit grayer, perhaps, but the movie nut pallor was still there; so was the underemployed movie-nut uniform — khakis, sneakers and grey sweatshirt.

At a nearby bar, Zellermeyer filled me in on the latest news. The personal news took only a few minutes. He had gotten married. Two years later he phoned his mother to tell her he thought he was married to an American spy. Rather than poison her, as his mother advised, he divorced her. The latest movie news took a lot longer. Zellermeyer's current position as editor of *Cinema Paradiso*, the D.O.A's weekly newsletter, allowed him to keep track of all that was happening at each of the Best Movie Scene clubs. The *Cinema Paradiso* was the periodical of choice for movie fans interested in movie club gossip. Zellermeyer's position gave him an inside look and allowed him to report on weddings, deaths, club outings, club mergers, and Turner Classic Movie listings of interest. For starters, he informed me that the D.O.A. had approved the request of the Best Neck Brace Scene Fan Club to share its clubhouse with the Best Business Card Scene Fan Club. The merger, prompted by the recession, worked much like a summer share in the Hamptons, with each fan club taking alternate weeks. The D.O.A., an acronym for Devotees of Film Art (the "F" being silent in homage to Edmond O'Brien, who was poisoned by a highball in a film of the same name), also approved the inclusion of movie scenes not mentioned in the original charter of each club. This cleared the way for movie scenes that did not exist 17 years ago when the clubs were formed. There was also a stipulation that barred any prospective new member who, for example, would say, "Why should I want to see a movie with Robert Ryan? Isn't he dead?" I totally agreed with the D.O.A. on this stipulation since I had seen Robert Ryan in the 72nd Street subway station three weeks after I read his obituary in the *New York Times*.

Zellermeyer also let me know that new categories had been added to the D.O.A. roster. These included best stuttering scenes, beach house scenes, library scenes, dueling scenes (inadvertently left out of my first book), whispering scenes, mine cave-in scenes and much more. After our drinks came, he handed me the complete list. He confided to me that during the extraordinary session of the D.O.A. to decide which scenes from the first edition should remain and which scenes in new categories should be added, there were two fistfights. The matter was resolved when it was decided that any best movie scene fan club that was unhappy with the final vote would be permitted to include a "Best Movie Recipe in Film History." The theory behind this is that while we know meals are eaten in movies, we rarely see them eaten. John Wayne would have starved on the meals we actually see him eating during the eighty-odd movies he made. We don't see Wayne dining on the screen because if directors had to show all the meals eaten in a movie, it would be ten hours long. (Meg Ryan in *When Harry Met Sally* is one of the exceptions.)

If not for my chance encounter with Zellermeyer, this book, and the spirit of compromise shown by the members of the D.O.A., could never have been written. As in my previous book, the film scenes within each category appear in no particular order.

Because I have always liked the hairdo James Whale gave Elsa Lanchester when he decided to build Frankenstein's monster a mate, I toyed with the idea of giving this companion piece the working title of "Bride of the 247 Best Movie Scenes in Film History." But cooler heads prevailed. So without counting the final number of movie scenes I had included, I simply called it *The 247 Best Movie Scenes in Film History Returns,* 2nd Edition. Or I would have had my publisher not counted the scenes and gently pointed out that I had actually described 549. And that's the number we used.

ACCOUNTANT

*It's a **Wonderful Life*** (1946). Probably the most woefully treated accountant in film history is Mr. Carter, the bank examiner from Elmira, New York, who is engaged to spend Christmas Eve looking over the books of Jimmy Stewart's Savings and Loan. He not only never gets to examine the books but also has to stay late into the night waiting for them and then forced to contribute a quarter to save Stewart from going to prison. Still, accountant scene fans persist in loving this scene if only because of the accountant sensibilities of the actor who played the role. (A check of both the screen credits and the shooting script failed to turn up his name.) Though director Frank Capra insisted on calling him a bank examiner, Carter's accountant presence was so strong, no one objected when the scene was placed in this category. That it won its award easily is already widely known in accountant scene fan circles.

The Producers (1974). Within the profession they have been whispered about for decades — those legendary accountants whose sharp auditing methods have forced clients into farfetched claims of poverty. One C.P.A. from Pittsburgh is reported to have caught a general ledger posting inaccuracy that made his client, the owner of a chain of fur salons, swear he was so poor his kitchen table only had three legs. This was the yardstick accountants measured themselves by until Mel Brooks got into the accounting business. Brooks created Neil Bloom (Gene Wilder), the sharp-eyed accountant who discovers that Max Bialistock raised $62,000 for a flop that cost only $60,000 to produce. The discovery set a new standard for accountant scenes, earned this particular example its place in film history, and created a new legend. Gene Wilder will be talked about in the profession for years to come as the accountant who made Zero Mostel say he was so poor he had to wear a cardboard belt.

Force of Evil (1948). In the accountant scene rulebook, appearance counts for a lot. Mr. Bauer (Thomas Gomez's accountant in the numbers bank he ran), looks like an accountant. He wears glasses, he is bald, he blends into the scenery, and most importantly, when he puts on his jacket, the back of it never touches his neck. In short, his accountant presence is so strong that accountant scene fans overlooked his breach of confidentiality when he squealed on Gomez, and voted him a place in accountant history.

Midnight Run (1988). He is known as "the accountant," both to the mob he embezzled $15 million from and to the accountant scene fan club. Though Charles Grodin (a.k.a. "the Duke") does not have the "look" of an accountant, he does have the sensibilities of one. So attuned is he to the accountant persona that he immediately understands that when a ten-year-old boy tells an embezzling accountant that he doesn't look like a criminal, he can always say, "I'm a white-collar criminal."

Moonstruck (1987). In an informal vote the membership elected Cher the prettiest accountant ever to balance the books in a movie.

ADOPTION

Tarzan Finds a Son (1939). Since Tarzan and Jane were not actually married, Hollywood had to find another way for them to have a baby. Remember, this was the 1930s. A plane crash with only one survivor, a baby boy, was the answer. Tarzan adopts him and names him Boy (wonderfully played by Johnny Sheffield). Proof that the adoption was a happy one is the scene where Boy and Tarzan and their sidekick chimpanzee, Cheetah, are having breakfast in their treehouse. As he and Boy share a laugh, Tarzan whispers something to Cheetah. Like *Lost in Translation* (2003), no one knows what Tarzan whispered but it must have been pretty funny because Cheetah burst out laughing.

Juno (2007). There's a sign pinned to the adoption scene fan club that says, "Vanessa, if you're still in, I'm still in. Juno." It's the note Ellen Page pins to Jennifer Garner's front door even though her dad doesn't want her to get ripped off by a couple of baby-starved "wing nuts." The scene adoption fans like most is when Jennifer picks up Juno's baby in the hospital for the first time and asks the nurse how she looks. The nurse replies, "Like you're scared shitless."

Superman: The Movie (1978). One of the most unusual adoption scenes happens after Glenn Ford's car swerves to avoid baby Superman's spaceship and gets a flat tire. As he's fixing it, the car collapses. Baby Superman gets out of the burning space capsule and lifts the car up so Ford can get out. That's when his wife asks Ford if they can keep the boy. "We can say he's the orphaned child of a cousin in North Dakota." Adoption scenes don't get much better than this.

E.T.: The Extra-Terrestrial (1982). More famous for its bicycle riding scenes, *E.T.* is really a story of adoption. Only in this case it's not a mother who adopts the stranded alien, but rather a ten-year-old boy named Elliott. Proof that the mother doesn't know there's an alien in her house is the scene when she opens a closet. E.T. is inside, disguised as a rag doll, and she doesn't even notice him. It's a favorite scene in the adoption fan clubhouse. Some of the more fanatical members sometimes wear rag doll wigs when they watch it.

The Jerk (1979). It's not only Stella who gets her groove back — Steve Martin got his back long before she did. The movie ends with the entire family dancing on the porch and singing "Pick a Bale of Cotton," with Martin dancing along, now having gained perfect rhythm. The joke throughout this very funny movie is that Martin thinks he is the natural son of the black sharecroppers, but adoption scene nuts know otherwise.

The Corn Is Green (1945). Adoption scene fans are quick to point out that adoptions give actors the chance to atone for their sins. As proof of this theory, they cite the scene where Bette Davis adopts Joan Loring's baby because she knows that John Dall would never leave for Oxford if he knew he was the father. So, even though she is a spinster school teacher, she takes the baby, giving thousands of movie nuts the chance to forgive her for not giving Herbert Marshall his heart medicine in *The Little Foxes* (1941).

Cheers for Miss Bishop (1941). Martha Scott needs no forgiveness, except maybe for not marrying William Gargan, who has loved her for 50 years. Still, when Scott adopts Mary Anderson's baby girl, even though Anderson had stolen the man she loved just before the wedding, it puts her one more level toward sainthood.

ALIEN TERMINATION

Alien (1979). Most movie nuts love to see bad, slimy aliens get wasted, but none so much as the members of the alien termination fan club. This is the movie that tops their list. As she prepares to enter stasis, Sigourney Weaver discovers that the Alien that ate its way out of John Hurt's stomach and killed every member of the crew is still aboard the shuttle. She puts on a space suit and opens the hatch, causing the shuttle to decompress, and forces the Alien to the open doorway. She shoots it with a grappling gun, which propels it outside, but the gun is yanked from her hands and catches in the closing door, tethering the Alien to the shuttle. It attempts to crawl into one of the engines, but Weaver activates them and blasts the Alien into space. She then puts herself and the cat into stasis for the return trip to Earth so she can rest up for the sequel, *Aliens* (1986).

Terminator 2: Judgment Day (1991). Few alien termination scenes are as satisfying as when Arnold Schwarzenegger fires that grenade at Robert Patrick, propelling the shape-shifting robot he portrays, formerly known as T-1000, into a vat of molten steel. The shot of Patrick screaming and melting while turning into all the people he has previously morphed into before he completely disintegrates was voted as the most exciting alien death scene ever. Fans of the Wicked Witch of the West would have liked Patrick to say, "I'm melting," but he doesn't have time.

Predator (1987). Arnold Schwarzenegger proves that his elimination of the T-1000 was no fluke when he terminates the extra-terrestrial that has been tracking and killing the members of his squad. Of course, the dumb alien has to challenge him to hand-to-hand combat first. This gives Arnold the chance to release the counterweight from one of his traps and a huge tree trunk falls on the alien, crushing him. Before the alien dies, Arnold asks him, "What are you?"

The alien asks Arnold the same question. We know the answer to that one: he's the terminator who killed the T-1000 and became the governor of California.

Independence Day (1996). After a dogfight with an alien pilot, Will Smith drags the alien from his spaceship and punches him, delivering his now famous line, "Welcome to Earth!" The scene where Smith and Jeff Goldblum plant the atomic bomb in the mother ship is pretty neat as well. The face of the alien leader when he sees the bomb's timer and realizes what will happen is very satisfying. The only mark against this movie is that after the shields are down, we only see the spaceships exploding and falling to earth. There's not one close-up of an alien termination.

ANT

Paths of Glory (1958). In this classic anti–ant-killing film from Stanley Kubrick, Ralph Meeker spots an ant crawling on the table in his makeshift jail cell. It is the evening before Meeker and Tim Carey are to be shot for cowardice. "You see that ant," Meeker says. "Tomorrow he'll be alive and we'll be dead." Carey looks at the ant, crushes it with his thumb, and says, "Now you got the edge on him." To many ant scene fans, it is the key scene in the film. Some people even believe Meeker is as much to blame as Carey for the ant's death because he revealed his deep-seated wish to change places with it. One gauge as to how much influence ant scene fans have in Hollywood is that neither Meeker nor Carey have worked in an ant film since.

The Naked Jungle (1957). Ant scene fans often point out that while the plot of this film revolves around a Brazilian ant army called a *marabunta*, it has a much deeper subtext, which reveals that it is really a film about antkind's desire to sail. Proof of this is the ants' final attack on Charlton Heston's plantation. When faced with a wide ditch of water surrounding the plantation, the army ants climb a tree to cut off leaves and then drop them to sailor ants waiting below. The sailor ants then make leaf boats and sail across the ditch. Ant scene auditors report that of the 7 trillion ant extras used in this film, nearly half knew how to sail leaves.

Them! (1954). Further proof that ants do not fare well on screen is this James Whitmore–Edmund Gwenn movie about mutant ants. At Gwenn's urging, the ant colonies are never given a chance to know that mankind meant them no harm as long as they behaved themselves. Instead, they are burned out of their desert colony and finally out of the storm drains of Los Angeles. An interesting footnote to the making of this film is that it was originally scheduled to be shot in Brooklyn, but the screenwriter and director didn't want the title of the film to be changed to "Dem."

No piece on ants in film should fail to mention the talents of Mel Blanc, an actor who knew his way around ant scenes. Blanc is the hero who created the ant-band sound that many of us have heard while watching cartoons as children. The sound can best be made by closing the mouth and going "eh-eh-eh-eh" through the nose.

ARITHMETIC

It's a Mad, Mad, Mad, Mad World (1963). There are always tears of joy in the eyes of arithmetic scene fan club members when Sid Caesar figures how to share the $350,000 buried under the big "W" seventeen different ways. A share for each of the four cars, which comes to $82,500 a car; a share for each person in the vehicle, which comes to $50,000 per person; and a share for each person who went down the ravine to watch Jimmy Durante kick the bucket, which comes to something else. But no matter how they figure it, there is always someone who doesn't like the way they figure it. So it becomes each man for himself, and as Buddy Hackett declares, "Good luck and may the best man win." Then he turns to Ethel Merman and says, "Except you, lady. May you just drop dead!"

Force of Evil (1948). So the syndicate that John Garfield heads can put all the small numbers banks out of business, he hires an arithmetic whiz to make the July 4 number to come out 776. In those days, the daily number was based on the last three digits of the amount of money bet that day at the race track. The arithmetic whiz has to bet enough money to make the handle come out 776, the number most gamblers play on Independence Day. He does his job, the number comes out 776, and the independent bookies go bankrupt. This puts the entire numbers operation under the syndicate. It all adds up to a fine arithmetic moment in a classic film noir, and one of Garfield's best performances.

Pi (1999). Arithmetic fans like movies that tell them mathematics is the language of nature. So when mathematician Sean Guilette learns from a Jewish mystic that the Torah is just a long string of numbers, they're overjoyed. When working on his computer, Guilette also finds a mathematical pattern in the stock market, and arithmetic junkies start brushing up on their multiplication tables. But by this point in the film Guilette's mind is so overloaded with numbers that he has a breakdown. In the final scene, when a little girl asks him to do a sum for her, Guilette tells her he doesn't do that anymore.

Good Will Hunting (1997). The blackboard in the arithmetic scene fan club lobby has the same advanced quantum physics problem that got Matt Damon recognized by a prize-winning physicist as a genius and landed him a date with Minnie Driver. No arithmetic aficionado has solved this problem yet, but neither has Minnie Driver showed up to watch them try.

The Maltese Falcon (1941). There's a good reason for the full-size photograph of Sydney Greenstreet that hangs over the arithmetic clubhouse fireplace. It's there because of the scene toward the end of the film in which Greenstreet figures out that he has been chasing the Falcon for 17 years, so one more year will be "an additional expenditure in time of only five and fifteen seventeenths percent." To arithmetic scene nuts, this scene is there to show that Greenstreet knows how to change a fraction into a decimal.

BABY

Small Change (1976). No one expects that François Truffaut would allow a baby playing with a cat by an open second-story windowsill to fall. But he does. Miraculously, the baby is unhurt. The secret, Truffaut is reported to have said, is to find a great stunt baby. This movie about the resilience of children is so charming, so irresistible, that baby scene fans do something they rarely ever do: they watch it until the very end.

The Untouchables (1987). Further proof of the importance of a good stunt baby is the scene in which Eliot Ness (Kevin Costner) and the other federal agents wait in Union Station to capture Al Capone's accountant. Brian De Palma sets up the scene by having Costner watching this woman trying to pull a baby carriage and two suitcases up the station stairs. Baby scene movie nuts are always at the edges of their seats during this sequence. The clock shows it is almost twelve; Capone's accountant will arrive any second. The woman keeps struggling up the stairs. The baby carriage is not one of those yuppie baby strollers — it is full size, the kind people put their babies in during the 1930s. Costner, annoyed that no one will help the poor woman, comes out of his hiding place and assists her. He can only use one hand because he has a shotgun in the other. When they are almost to the top, the accountant and his bodyguards appear. One of them spots Costner and he is forced to let go of the baby carriage and shoot the bodyguard. The baby carriage then begins to roll down the steps. The stunt baby is smiling. The gunfight begins. The carriage is rolling, the mother is screaming and bullets are flying. Andy Garcia, one of the agents, stops the carriage before it kills the baby stuntman and shoots the bodyguard who threatens to shoot the accountant. De Palma blatantly stole the baby carriage idea from the silent film *The Battleship Potemkin* (1925), only Eisenstein's budget didn't include money for a stunt baby so they had to use a real one.

A Beautiful Mind (2001). To show other movie nuts they are not hardhearted, the baby scene fan club limited their baby-in-danger scenes to three. This third baby-in-danger scene, and a pretty good one, is when Russell Crowe goes upstairs with his baby to give it a bath. But he has one of his hallucinations and leaves the baby unattended with the bathwater running. Crowe's wife (Jennifer Connelly), sensing something is wrong, runs up the stairs and gets the baby out of the water just in time.

Baby Boom (1987). On a lighter note, there are the scenes with Baby Elizabeth, the toddler Diane Keaton inherits from a distant cousin whom she hasn't seen in years. The best scene occurs after Keaton turns down millions for her baby-food applesauce and comes back to Vermont. Elizabeth, who is playing on the floor, looks up at Keaton in the doorway, smiles, and says, "Mommy!"

Look Who's Talking (1989). This movie did not get a single vote in the best baby scene ballot. Cute, wise-cracking babies with the voice of Bruce Willis (and other actors) commenting on life from a baby's point of view cause projectile vomiting among baby scene movie nuts. Ditto for *Look Who's Talking Too* (1990).

BAD TEACHERS

The Bad Teachers Union has forbidden any member of the bad teachers fan club to list scenes portraying teachers who are bad. To sidestep this ruling, a small cabal of best teacher movie nuts listed their favorite actors in a bad teacher movie role and sent the final tally anonymously to *Cinema Paradiso*. They are, in no particular order of preference: Robert Donat, in *Goodbye Mr. Chips* (1939), for his beautifully sub-par teaching performance before he married Greer Garson; Burt Reynolds, in *Starting Over* (1979), for not realizing he needed a full hour's material before he came to class, not the five minutes he had prepared (although he did promise to be better prepared next time); Dennis Quaid, in *Smart People* (2007), for always writing on the blackboard with his back to his class until Sarah Jessica Parker told him to make eye contact with his class once in a while; and Morton Lowry, in *How Green Was My Valley* (1941), for his role as the brutal school teacher who was so nasty to Roddy McDowall, and who thoroughly deserved to get punched out by the blind boxer, Dai Bando (Rhys Williams). Finally, there is the wonderfully foul-mouthed Cameron Diaz in *Bad Teacher* (2011), who, when asked the day before school starts if she's excited about the next day, responds with, "Why? Is it Saturday?" But it is when she gets to class that Diaz truly becomes the best bad teacher in movie history. She tells a student who doesn't think she knows very much, "I'll tell you what I know. A kid who wears the same gym sweatshirt three days a week isn't getting laid until he's 29. That's what I know."

BALLET

The Red Shoes (1948). Ballet scene movie nuts love it when Anton Walbrook asks Moira Shearer why she wants to dance. "Why do you want to live?" she responds. "Because I must," Walbrook replies. So it is with ballet scene aficionados, who must watch the scene where the red ballet shoes that

Shearer is wearing force her to jump off that balcony in front of an approaching train and then listen as she weakly asks Marius Goring to take them off.

The Story of Three Loves (1953). Sure, Moira Shearer is a beautiful dancer, but she rarely makes it out of a ballet movie alive. In "The Jealous Lover" segment of this three-part movie, Shearer, who has a heart condition, cannot live unless she dances, but if she dances, she won't live. She does dance and she doesn't live. Heart attack fans didn't claim the scene where she collapses on the staircase because Bette Davis (*The Little Foxes*) wasn't there to not get her heart medicine.

The Turning Point (1977). This is the movie that made it okay for ballet movie nuts to admit they are ballet movie nuts. What clinched it was Mikhail Baryshnikov's soaring jumps during his solo in *Don Quixote*. When talking about this film, ballet scene fans have been heard to say, "I think this one is going to do it for us." They are paraphrasing what Anne Bancroft said to Deedee (Shirley MacLaine) when MacLaine asked Bancroft how her daughter was doing in the company: "I think she's going to do it for you, Deedee."

Black Swan (2010). Scary. Confusing. Painful to watch. These were some of the more favorable comments from the membership of the ballet scene fan club. They liked Natalie Portman's acting and her dance double's dancing, but remained in the dark about how all that blood got on Portman's tutu in the final act. All, however, agree that Barbara Hershey's performance as a ballet mom deserved a few extra curtain calls. But if you're at a bar with a ballet movie nut, don't try to compare this film to *The Red Shoes*.

Tales of Hoffman (1951). At the opening of each ballet scene fan club meeting, the president raps his gavel and says, "If there are any opera scene fans present, you have read the schedule incorrectly. This is not your month to screen this film." The announcement is a result of an agreement between opera and ballet movie nuts to screen this film on alternative months. The decision to call it a ballet movie was based on the presence of Moira Shearer and Robert Helpmann. What made it an opera movie was the music of Jacques Offenbach. The fight between the two categories was a long, contentious one, but when Moira Shearer emerged from the meeting and raised the historic agreement over her beautiful red hair, announcing, "Peace in our time," the matter was settled.

Fantasia (1940). The word among members of the ballet scene fan club is that the ostriches are more graceful than the elephants, especially the principal ostrich, who wears a pink bow on her head (the rest of the company wears blue). The elephants are pretty good, too, but only slightly better than the hippos, who dance a lot better than the alligators. The membership all agreed that the Dance of the Hours from *La Giocanda* is the perfect music for animated animals who dance in tutus. Unfortunately, the ballet scenes in this movie never came to the floor for a vote. That's because Tea Party ballet nuts wouldn't compromise on the principle of no animated ballet scenes until deeper cuts were made in the ballet scene fan club budget.

BALLOON

Strangers on a Train (1951). Balloon scene fans are not full of hot air when they speculate that when someone bursts a kid's balloon, it foreshadows murder. They point to the neat little balloon scene that got overlooked by many balloon scene nuts too engrossed in the criss-cross murder plot devised by the psychotic Robert Walker. On his way to murder Farley Granger's wife, Walker passes a kid carrying a balloon. The kid must have looked at Walker the wrong way because Walker takes the cigarette he's smoking and bursts the balloon. Or maybe that's something all criss-cross wife murderers do before they commit murder, because right after Walker punctures the balloon, he follows Granger's wife onto that island and calmly strangles her.

Up (2009). A scene in which thousands of helium-filled balloons lift a house and fly it to South America would have won hands down had it not been a Pixar animation film. So it ran for purse money only. Balloon scene fans find it interesting that though the main character, Carl, was voiced by Ed Asner, the guy on screen looked an awful lot like Spencer Tracy.

An American Werewolf in London (1981). Henry Hull could never have done it. It took an American werewolf from N.Y.U. to pull off what admirers of this genre refer to as a classic balloon heist. Hiding naked behind a bush in a London park, David Naughton lures a little boy over so he can steal his balloons in order to wear them as underwear. Though the scene lasts but a few seconds and has little to do with the plot, it won its place on the list because it resulted in a line of dialogue that will be remembered as long as there are balloon enthusiasts left who speak the English language. It is delivered with just the right amount of matter-of-factness by the English boy to his mother: "A naked American man stole my balloons."

The Third Man (1950). A temporary restraining order was lifted by the D.O.A., which allowed balloon fans to award this scene its place in balloon history. Here are the crucial elements of the sequence: Trevor Howard, his sergeant and half the Austrian police force are waiting in the Vienna night to spring the trap on Orson Welles. There are footsteps, then a shadow appears on the far side of the square. It gets bigger and bigger as the man approaches. It is not Welles, but an old man selling balloons. He walks up to Trevor Howard and, in the deepest bass voice yet to be heard in a balloon scene, says, "Bahl-LOON? Bahl-LOON, mein Herr?" It turns out Howard doesn't want a balloon, but the sergeant buys one just to get rid of the balloon vendor.

That, essentially, is the scene and those are the facts on which the decision to lift the restraining order were based. The two reasons the order was lifted were as follows: The first sighting of the balloon vendor was indeed a shadow, but it was a balloon shadow. Moreover, there was only one shadow, but there were 14 balloons. The second and stronger reason is that when the balloon man speaks, he doesn't say, "sha-DOW"—he says, "bahl-LOON!"

Kind Hearts and Coronets (1949). A recent ruling by the D.O.A. allowing hot air balloon scenes to be included in this category paved the way for the scene in which Dennis Price shoots an arrow at Lady Agatha's hot air balloon from his window. Lady Agatha (Alec Guinness), a suffragette, is tossing pamphlets from her gondola as she flies over London. We never see Price's arrow hit the balloon, but we know it does because Price smiles, then leans out the window and slowly looks down.

There are a number of actors who have showed a partiality for balloons. Standing out among them are Peter Lorre, who had the good taste to buy one for his little victims in the German thriller, *M* (1931), and Danny Kaye, who in *Merry Andrew* (1958) preferred to wear his balloons inside his trousers.

BALLPOINT PEN

Breaking Away (1979). Whenever they are asked whether ballpoint pens are really important in the grand scheme of things, admirers of ballpoint pen scenes invariably cite this charmer directed by Peter Yates. The scene they always point to is the one in which Paul Dooley removes the fourteen ballpoint pens from his shirt pocket before making love to Barbara Barrie. They conclude that if Dooley hadn't removed those pens, Dennis Christopher would still be an only child.

Are ballpoint pen scenes important? Indeed! "As important as procreation!" cry ballpoint pen enthusiasts across the country.

Viva Zapata! (1952). The inclusion of the scene in which Mexican dictator Porfirio Díaz circles Emiliano Zapata's name for asking a question about boundary markers is testimony to the stubbornness of ballpoint pen fans. Díaz couldn't possibly have been using a ballpoint, since the film depicts events that took place in 1910, and the ballpoint pen was not in use until about 1940. Ballpoint pen lawyers point out that this line of reasoning is full of holes. They admit that the events in the film took place in 1910, but contend that the film was actually made in 1952, twelve years after ballpoints were in use. Ballpointers further argue that a ballpoint pen was used in this scene because neither Elia Kazan, the film's director, nor Marlon Brando, its star, were sticklers for historical pen accuracy. When asked to verify this theory, no one at 20th Century–Fox, the studio that made the film, was available for comment. Which leaves us with this question: It's a great scene, but is it a great ballpoint pen scene?

Rain Man (1988). Many ballpoint pen scene fans still believe that a large part of the credit for Dustin Hoffman's Oscar for his performance in this film should go to the ballpoint pens he always carried in his shirt pocket. This doesn't necessarily mean they consider ballpoint pens in the pocket to be a lucky talisman for an actor. Nor was it the reason they voted to include this film on the award list. It was Hoffman's ballpoint pen loyalty and his insistence on not leaving wherever he happened to be without them that really counted when the ballots were cast.

Nerds in Paradise (1987). The rumor that ballpoint pen fans passed up *Revenge of the Nerds* (1984) because they didn't like the nerd image projected by a plastic case filled with ballpoint pens is totally without substance. The fans have consistently pointed out that ballpoint pens do not judge the character of the person in whose pocket they happen to find themselves. They are also the first to admit that there are a number of scenes in the earlier film in which ballpoints appear but feel that none are worthy of this award. With the selection of this nerd sequel, they hope the "nerd image" rumor will be finally laid to rest.

Ballpoint pen people feel the chosen scene is not only worthy of an award but also quite moving. It occurs in the final moments of the film, when a former campus jock (the guy the nerds saved when he was marooned on the island) is initiated into the nerd fraternity and presented with his plastic case containing 10 ballpoint pens. What endears this scene to ballpoint pen fans is that he really seems proud to receive it.

BANK ROBBERY

Take the Money and Run (1969). Before you plan to rob a bank, it's a good idea to practice your penmanship. Woody Allen finds this out when the teller thinks the note he hands over says, "I am pointing a 'gub' at you." Allen has to tell him the word is "gun." The note is passed around until it gets to the bank guard, who then arrests Allen. But first Allen has to phone his girlfriend to tell her that he can't make it tonight, although he promises to give her a call in about 10 years.

Butch Cassidy and the Sundance Kid (1969). Paul Newman and Robert Redford experience similar communication problems when they try to rob a bank in Bolivia. They can't make anyone understand them because they don't speak Spanish. This is why there's a photo of Katharine Ross over the teller cage reproduction in the main room of the bank robbery scene aficionados' clubhouse: she's the one who taught them to say "hands up and face the wall" in Spanish.

The Dark Knight (2008). It is well known among bank robbery scene fans that the advertisement that the Joker (Heath Ledger) placed in the help-wanted section of the *New York Times* under "Bank Robbers" received no replies. The reason could be that in the bank robbery scene which opens this film, Ledger downsizes the robbers who helped him on the bank job by shooting them.

The Thomas Crown Affair (1968). A pretty neat daytime bank robbery. It's on the list because nobody gets hurt, and the bank robbers don't even know each other. The red smoke is a nice touch, as is how the gang gets rid of the money by dumping it in a cemetery trash can. However, in an informal poll, bank robbery scene aficionados agreed they could have done without all those split screen shots.

Raising Arizona (1987). Bank robbery fans did not vote this film in because it is one of the funniest bank robbery scenes they have ever watched. They voted it in because it is the only bank robbery in movie history in which the bank robbers take along a baby. There's also a nice little exchange between Nicolas Cage and one of the bank customers. When Cage tells him, "Freeze and get on the floor," the customer responds, "Now which is it? Do you want us to freeze or get on the floor?"

BAR ROOM

My Darling Clementine (1946). The bar scene in this John Ford western didn't make the best bar room list for having drinks sliding down one end of the bar to the other (though it does have one of those, with Victor Mature doing the sliding), but rather because it has the best bar room line in movie history. Wyatt Earp (Henry Fonda) leans across the bar and asks Mac the bar-man (J. Farrell MacDonald) if he's ever been in love and Mac delivers the line that puts this great scene over the top: "Nope. I've been a bartender all my life."

Lost in Translation (2003). The bar scene in this luxury Tokyo hotel didn't make the best bar scene list because Bill Murray was drinking the top-shelf scotch that he was paid two million dollars to advertise. Nor did it win

It was Henry Fonda's crush on Clementine that made him ask Mac the barman if he had ever been in love in *My Darling Clementine* (1946).

because Scarlett Johansson sends him over a drink. Nor did it win because the tuxedo Murray was wearing was still pinned in the back from his photo shoot. It won because I happened to be present during the voting and, as a member of Best Cigar Scenes in Film History Fan Club, recognized the Bolivar Corona Gigante that Murray was smoking. So, movie fans, it was me (make that, it was I) who cast the deciding vote.

Star Wars, Episode IV (1977). I could swear there's a bar in Bodega Bay, California, that's modeled after the Cantina. But the scene actually made the list because when R2D2 enters the bar, the bartender tells him, "We don't serve droids here!" That the line is translated at the bottom of the screen into some unknown alien language is a nice touch, as is the fact that the band (looking like hung-over ghosts rather than gorillas) reminds me a lot of the Nairobi Trio from the 1950s Ernie Kovacs show. Had Kovacs still been alive when this movie was released, I have the feeling he would have claimed copyright infringement.

Cocktail (1988). Tom Cruise must have a terrific memory because not once in this film, despite all the drinks he serves, do we ever see him ring up a tab. No wonder the bar he works behind is always crowded.

The bar scene in the 1953 western *Shane* had a great bar room brawl (Alan Ladd and Van Heflin taking on six pretty tough-looking cowhands), but it was not included because Ladd ordered a bottle of sarsaparilla and not a shot of whiskey.

The arrival of the latest *Cinema Paradiso* bi-weekly emptied the club-house bar and sent bar room scene aficionados rushing for their YouTubes. What caused the sudden exodus (the noun, not the movie) was Arnold Zellermeyer's blistering review of the first bar room scene in film history. The plot seems to be about a drunkard who can't find the door and is helped out of the bar by two other drunks. The short film, called *Cripple Creek*, is reported to have been shot by Thomas Alva Edison in 1899.

BASEBALL

The Natural (1984). Okay, Robert Redford may have been too old to play a college student in *The Way We Were*, but he's not too old to play the oldest rookie in baseball in this wonderful film. And even though Tom Hanks claims there's no crying in baseball, the tears in the baseball scene clubhouse start to flow when Roy Hobbs breaks his bat, Wonderboy, on a foul ball in the last game of the season. Muffled sobs can be heard when Redford tells the batboy who idolizes him to "go pick me out a winner, Bobby." The movie audience knows something great is about to happen when we get a shot of the young pitcher taking the sign, a shot of Glenn Close watching Redford from the stands, and then a shot of the baseball slowing down after the pitch. Something great does happen. Redford hits that amazing home run that short-circuits the electric system and sends sparks flying everywhere. Close is crying with joy as Redford slowly rounds the bases; the Knights have won the pennant and Wilfred Bromley can hang on to his team. But before the members in the baseball scene clubhouse can dry their eyes, the screen fades to black and there's a shot of Hobbs playing catch with the son he never knew he had. A beautiful ending to a fine film.

A flood of tears always begins in the baseball scene clubhouse when Robert Redford breaks his favorite bat (Wonderboy) in *The Natural* (1984).

Field of Dreams (1989). If you're a movie fan who considers that game of catch Kevin Costner has with his father to be one of the great baseball scenes of all time, you're not alone — so do most of the members of the baseball scene fan club. Midwesterners in the fan club particularly like it when Costner's dad asks him, "Is this heaven?" "No," Costner says. "It's Iowa."

Bull Durham (1988). Baseball movie nuts love Susan Sarandon because she never sleeps with a player hitting under .250 ... unless he has a lot of RBIs. They also love this movie because it lets fans know what players really talk about when the catcher goes to the mound. Costner, the catcher, wants to know what the players are talking to the pitcher about and goes out there to investigate. It turns out they are discussing what wedding present they should get for one of the players who is about to get married. It's the shortstop who suggests candlesticks. Costner has a nice little baseball scene when the pitcher, Tim Robbins, keeps shaking him off because he wants to throw a fastball and Costner wants a curve. So Costner gives in, but lets the batter know what the next pitch will be and the batter smashes it out of the park.

Pride of the Yankees (1942). The beauty of baseball is that it can be slow moving. So is this film. Baseball doesn't get a lot of screen time here, but baseball movie nuts consider Lou Gehrig's line, "Today, I consider myself the luckiest man on the face of the earth," to be the best baseball quote in film history.

Bang the Drum Slowly (1973). Further proof that catchers make for interesting baseball moments on screen is this touching film. Robert De Niro plays a dumb catcher dying of Hodgkin's disease. Michael Moriarty is the pitcher who helps him get through the season. The final scene of De Niro struggling to catch a foul pop-up for the last out is heartbreaking and wonderful.

The Great Escape (1963). Who says great baseball scenes have to be played on a baseball diamond? Not Steve McQueen. All McQueen needs is a ball and a mitt. Baseball scene nuts never fail to respond to the wistful expression on the young German guard's face as he walks away from the "cooler" after he locks McQueen up and hears the sound of McQueen throwing the baseball against the wall.

From the sports page of the August 2 edition of *Cinema Paradiso*: The annual softball game between the Baseball Scene Red Sox and Neck Brace Scene White Sox was held at the Little League field in Montauk, Long Island. The score was Neck Brace White Sox, 14; Baseball Scene Red Sox, 5. The score was payback for neck brace scene fans because it reversed the 21–2 drubbing Ralph Waite received when he played a game of ping pong (while wearing a neck brace) with Jack Nicholson in *Five Easy Pieces*.

BATHTUB

Diabolique (1955). Bathtubs must really enjoy playing a big role in horror films. In this black-and-white thriller from France, a wife (Vera Clouzot) and a mistress (Simone Signoret) drown Paul Meurisse in a bathtub, then toss him in the pool to make it look like an accident. But the body never floats to the surface and is nowhere to be found when the pool is drained. It turns up again in the bathtub, and when it rises, the wife, who has a weak heart, collapses and dies. So what we have here is a bathtub setup. Meurisse was never dead and had planned his fake death with Signoret. But before the pair can escape, they are arrested, proving there is justice in bathtub movies.

Fatal Attraction (1987). Glenn Close gets a splash of bathtub justice in this neat thriller. The actress who made the phrase "I will not be ignored" famous is nearly drowned in the bathtub. But this time, when she rises from the bathwater, Ann Archer shoots her dead. Members of the bathtub scene fan club take full credit for the drop in infidelity the year this film was released.

How Green Was My Valley (1941). Footbath pans are not bathtubs. This was the ruling by the D.O.A. As a result, the footbath that Donald Crisp was taking when he was visited by the mine owner to ask if his son could call on Maureen O'Hara couldn't officially be counted in the final vote. Nor could it be placed in the marriage proposal category; fathers asking permission for a son to call on another father's daughter do not count. So what is it? It is simply one of many lovely scenes in what many movie lovers consider the best American movie ever made.

Cowboy (1958). This long forgotten bathtub gem shows that a Chicago hotel clerk who goes on a cattle drive can become tough enough to sit in a bathtub, fire his six-shooter at a fly on the wall and hit it. Glenn Ford and Jack Lemmon are wonderful, though Lemmon, who hated riding horses, said this was probably the only western he would ever do in his film career. He kept his word.

The Cincinnati Kid (1965). The odds on a full house losing to a straight flush in a two-handed game of five-card stud poker are more than 45 million to one. The odds on Tuesday Weld giving you a bath while telling you about a French movie she saw with Ann-Margret are even higher. Sure, this is a poker movie, but don't tell that to bathtub movie nuts.

Will Penny (1968). Bathtub scene fans wanted to list this underrated western in this category but their by-laws prevented them from doing so. Notable bathtub scenes are for murder and relaxation, not to freshen up. Charlton Heston only took his bath because the lovely Joan Hackett told him he stank.

BEACH HOUSE

Something's Gotta Give (2003). Followers of beach house movies probably don't know that Sand People (from *Star Wars, Episode IV*) always walk in single file to hide their numbers, but they all know that after a heart attack the rule of thumb in the Hamptons is that if you can walk up the stairs from the beach to the beach house, you can have sex. That's what Jack Nicholson tries to do in this very satisfying beach house film that has not only a beautiful Hamptons beach house but also Diane Keaton performing one of the funniest crying scenes ever. It should be noted that after the film's release, sales of Hamptons beach houses doubled. Nicholson's and Keaton's salaries probably did as well.

The Ghost Writer (2010). The Martha's Vineyard beach house in this very neat thriller may look like a fortress on the outside, but inside there are pretty good views, good sandwiches (served by the Asian housekeeper) and good scotch, most of it downed by the film's star Ewan McGregor. Things get tricky when McGregor learns that Roman Polanski, the film's director, isn't allowed in the United States and much of the film was shot on Sylt, part of an island chain in the North Sea. It gets trickier still when he learns that Pierce Brosnan's wife works for the CIA. McGregor barely makes it to the end of the film. He then gets run over by a car. Nice beach house, though, wherever it is located.

A Star Is Born (1954). The lesson in this fine musical is to never build a beach house too close to the ocean. Judy Garland never learns that. So when her husband Norman Mane (James Mason) overhears Garland tell Charles Bickford that she is giving up her career to devote herself to Mason, he tells Garland that he's going for a swim and drowns himself. The last line in the film, "Hello everybody. This is Mrs. Norman Mane," is a real crowd pleaser.

BICYCLE

Butch Cassidy and the Sundance Kid (1969). Paul Newman did his own stunts, Katharine Ross enjoyed the ride on the handlebars and "Raindrops Keep Falling on My Head" isn't a bad song either. Bicycle scene fans enjoy Newman riding backward and crashing into the fence even more than all the gunplay.

Pee-Wee's Big Adventure (1965). You have to love a movie where Pee-Wee Herman wakes up from a dream in which he and his bike have won the Tour de France. Pee-Wee loves his bike more than anything else in the world. It's red and white and kept in a special garage with a spotlight that shines on it when Pee-Wee opens the door. He won't sell it for all the money in the world — not for a hundred, trillion, billion dollars. When it's stolen, he is told by a psychic that his bike is hidden in the Alamo and he sets out to find it. Bike fans are quickly bored by all the stuff that happens to Pee-Wee along the way and usually can be seen leaving the theater. But they always return to watch Pee-Wee get his bike back.

Breaking Away (1979). Bicycle scene nuts find it odd that a movie about a bicycle race should be better known for its ballpoint pen scene, in which Paul Dooley signifies he wants to make love to his wife, Barbara Barrie, by removing the ballpoint pens from his pocket. To remedy the false labeling of this film as a ballpoint pen movie, bike fans point to the wonderful scene where Dennis Christopher races a truck along the highway when he is training for his race against the Italian bicycle team. He beats the truck but doesn't have much luck with the Italians. When he passes them, they stick a wrench in his back wheel. The wonderful Italian opera music adds a lot to these scenes. The film won an Academy Award for best original screenplay for Steve Tesich. Tesich went on to write the script for *American Flyers* (1985), but that movie wasn't so hot. Maybe it was Kevin Costner's mustache. Shortly after he shaved it off he became a superstar.

E.T.: The Extra-Terrestrial (1982). E.T. may be wrapped in a white towel but he still knows how to make a bicycle airborne. Not the corny scene where 10-year-old Elliott and E.T. ride across the moon, but the scene where the neighborhood gang is trying to elude the police and E.T. lifts all of them into the sky. Pretty neat.

The Bicycle Thief (1948). Pee-Wee Herman should be forced to watch this movie. Lamberto Maggiorani doesn't love his bicycle as much as he needs it for his job of putting up posters of Rita Hayworth. But it is stolen on his first day at work. The entire film is about Maggiorani and his son searching the streets of Rome for the stolen bike. Critics have called this film by Vittorio DeSica one of the greatest films of all time. To a bike scene fan, it is simply a great bike movie.

The Great Escape (1963). Bicycle scene aficionados never wonder how James Coburn happens to have a wire cutter on him after he escapes from a German P.O.W. camp. All they care about is that the bicycle he steals allows him to be one of the prisoners who safely escapes.

BIRD

How Green Was My Valley (1941). This simple tale of how a bird helps Roddy McDowall to walk again is often referred to as a bird classic. Walter Pidgeon sets the key scene up when he tells Roddy that he will walk again by spring. That's because Roddy is bedridden after falling through the ice to save his mother (Sara Algood) from drowning.

The scene that has bird scene enthusiasts all atwitter occurs when Roddy is lying in bed by an open window. At the door, his mother and sister (Maureen O'Hara) are watching. A bird flies by and lands on the windowsill. Roddy looks at the bird, then at his mother, and utters what many consider to be the most dramatic line of the film. In a voice filled with hope and bird love, Roddy asks, "Spring?" After a few drinks, bird scene lovers, who do not usually make light of bird scenes, are likely to remark that if the bird hadn't landed on the windowsill, Roddy would never have been able to make *Planet of the Apes*.

Mon Oncle (1958). The great Jacques Tati's bird sensibilities were so highly developed that he instinctively knew the canary in the courtyard below wouldn't sing unless the sun shone on it. Each morning, before Tati left his apartment, he fixed his balcony window at a special angle so that the sun would reflect off it and on to the canary. This not only pleased the canary, who then began to sing, but also delighted bird scene lovers, who thought the scene so inventive they made its selection unanimous.

Broadway Danny Rose (1984). In great bird scenes, like great cigar scenes, birds need not appear on screen. They merely have to be talked about with feeling. Such is the case when the actor with the bird act complains to Woody Allen that a cat ate his lead act, "Peewee, the Bird." The fact that an actor was holding Peewee's empty bird cage during the scene may have weighed heavily in the voting. Like cigar scene fans, bird scene fans understand that in the making of an exhilarating bird scene, bird yearning counts for a lot.

The Birds (1963). With so many bird scenes to choose from in this Alfred Hitchcock heart-stopper about bird revenge, bird scene enthusiasts chose one that is actually funny. It occurs near the beginning of the film as Tippi Hedren is taking the two lovebirds to Rod Taylor. The cage is on the floor of her sports car on the passenger side, and the birds are facing forward. As Hedren drives along the twisty coast highway, the camera, at floor level, shows the two birds leaning in the direction of each turn. When the car turns left, the birds lean left. When the car turns right, the birds lean right. It is classic Hitchcock.

To those who ask, "Why wasn't a more exciting scene chosen? The school children running down the hill being attacked by birds, or the birds flying down Rod Taylor's chimney?," the answer is quite simple. Many bird scene fans are also bird lovers and they don't like to reward scenes that show birds in a bad light.

Dumbo (1941). One needn't be an avid bird scene fan to know that when one sees a crow smoking a cigar talking to an elephant in a tree, one can expect a bird scene that is considerably above the average. Walt Disney does not let us down. When the crows find Dumbo sleeping on a branch and sing, "Did you ever see an elephant fly," bird scene fans wonder if the delight they receive can be topped. They soon have their answer when the crows give Dumbo a magic feather, push him off the cliff and fly with him, singing, "I've seen everything when I've seen an elephant fly."

Though it isn't generally known, a claim was put in for this scene by cigar scene fans, but it was quietly withdrawn when it became clear that it would be too difficult to judge the quality of an animated cigar.

The Maltese Falcon (1941). When the members of the Best Bird Scene Fan Club voted down the scene in which Sydney Greenstreet unwraps the newspaper that the black bird is packed in and begins stabbing at it with his penknife, crying, "It's a fake. It's a fake!," they did so because the Maltese Falcon was not a real bird. Rule #1 in the criteria for establishing the best bird scenes states this in no uncertain terms.

Visitors to the bird scene clubhouse in Oxnard, California, might be intrigued by the green parrot displayed on the mantle. It is reported to be the stuffed remains of the parrot who flew around the deck of Douglas Fairbanks's ship in *Sinbad the Sailor* (1947) screeching, "Jamal, Jamal!" The parrot, a favorite of bird scene fans, was trying to tell Fairbanks that Jamal was really Walter Slezak before they reached the island of Derriabar. That the parrot is indeed the same bird as that used in the film was proven conclusively at a recent viewing of the film. In the final scene, when Slezak's eyes turn brilliant green after he drinks the poison he had intended for Fairbanks, the stuffed parrot was held next to the screen and shown to be the same shade of green.

BLACKMAIL

Bride of Frankenstein (1935). When Dr. Pretorius needs Henry Frankenstein to help him create a companion for Boris Karloff, he blackmails him into it. After kidnapping Frankenstein's girlfriend, the beautiful Valerie Hobson, he promises to release her only if Frankenstein helps him. To prove

Hobson is alive, he lets Frankenstein speak to her over the cell phone he has invented. That added bonus is said to be the first cell phone scene in movie history. As of at this writing, there is no cell phone scene fan club to claim the scene as their own.

American Beauty (1999). When it looks as if Kevin Spacey is about to get fired from his job, what he says to his boss to get a full year's severance and medical benefits was voted the best blackmailing line in movie history: "Can you prove you didn't offer to save my job if you blow me?"

The Best Man (1964). Blackmailing scene fans were so disappointed that Henry Fonda was too nice to use the information on Cliff Robertson that would have put Robertson out of the running for the presidential nomination that they now refer to Fonda as "that blackmailing wimp."

Crimes and Misdemeanors (1989). Never blackmail an ophthalmologist. That's the lesson Angelica Huston fails to learn when she tries to blackmail Martin Landau into leaving his wife by threatening to expose their affair. Landau arranges for a hit man to do her in and he lives happily ever after. Woody Allen isn't so lucky, since Mia Farrow, the woman he's in love with, marries the guy who fired him.

Victim (1962). Dirk Bogarde is pretty good as a barrister trying to expose a blackmailing ring preying on male homosexuals in 1950s London. However, the club agreed that though it is always nice to see Dennis Price, the film is not so hot, and so the movie didn't make the best blackmailing scene final cut.

BODY IN CAR TRUNK

White Heat (1949). The one thing you should never tell Cody Jarrett (Jimmy Cagney) after he throws you in the trunk of a car is "It's stuffy in here. I need some air." Because as sure as shooting, Cagney is going to give you some air by pulling a gun from his pants and blasting four bullet holes into the trunk.

Psycho (1960). Norman Bates has a lot more in common with Cody Jarrett than just being a mother-fixated psychotic killer: he also likes to put bodies in car trunks. Members of the body in car trunk fan club usually fast-forward through the shower scene so they can watch Anthony Perkins push Janet Leigh's car into the lake. They always root for the car to sink.

Goodfellas (1990). If there's one lesson actors who portray bodies in a car trunk have learned, it is that if you've been battered to a pulp and find yourself wrapped in a tablecloth lying inside one, don't bang on the trunk. If you do, Joe Pesci, Robert De Niro and Ray Liotta will stop the car, raise the lid, and then stab you and shoot you until you really are dead.

The Hangover (2009). Banging on the car trunk worked out a lot better for Ken Jeong, the naked Asian who pops out of the trunk and beats up Bradley Cooper, Zach Galifianakis and Ed Helms with a tire jack. Members rank it as the funniest car trunk scene in movie history. They are happy that when Galifianakis tells Jeong he hates Godzilla, it doesn't prevent him from getting zonked.

Wonder Boys (2000). There is no rule in the body in car trunk fan club that says the body in the trunk can't be a dead one-eyed dog. Like Michael Douglas says before he puts it into his car, "The dog is dead. Believe me. I know a dead dog when I see one." There is never a dry eye in the clubhouse when Tobey Maguire shoots the mutt and helps Douglas hide it in the trunk of his car. Didn't he bite Douglas in the leg for no apparent reason (other than the fact that Douglas was having an affair with Frances McDormand, the wife of Richard Thomas, the dog's owner)? The charms of this underappreciated film are such that most body in car trunk fans stay to watch the entire film.

Though there aren't a lot of body in a car trunk scenes in film history to choose from, fans had the good sense to leave out the one in *Bounty Hunter* (2010). The vote was unanimous. Sure, Gerard Hunter throws Jennifer Aniston into the trunk of his car. But that does not help. Even if it had been a good body in a car trunk scene, which it isn't, the members of the body in a car trunk fan club always consider the movie in which the scene appears and they consider this film to be the worst romantic comedy ever made.

BRAIN TUMOR

Hannah and Her Sisters (1986). Brain tumor fans were taken completely by surprise when, of all the actors in this film, it was Woody Allen himself who got the chance to play a character with a suspected brain tumor. There were many who felt that Mia Farrow would have been a better choice (all those kids without a mom). And Lloyd Nolan would have looked infinitely better going under the CAT scan device. But no, Allen kept the suspected tumor for himself, causing some brain tumor fans to openly accuse the film's writer/director of "brain tumor selfishness."

Though Allen gave himself some pretty good symptoms, such as loss of hearing in one ear and a spot on an X-ray, he left out suspicious smells, which didn't matter anyway since it turned out he didn't have a brain tumor after all. The small group of brain tumor fans who felt it unfair that Allen survived with his "brain tumor" while Bette Davis died from hers voted to keep this film off the list. Their sentiments kept the vote close, but did not change the final result.

Dark Victory (1939). Brain tumor fans point to this movie whenever they need to prove their theory that the rich have better brain tumor symptoms than the rest of us. Two of Bette Davis's more interesting symptoms are losing a bundle of money at bridge (because of an inability to concentrate) and experiencing double vision when the horse she is riding is about to jump a fence.

Unhappily, even though Davis is married to a brain surgeon (George Brent), she never makes it out of her brain tumor scene alive. Her death is peaceful enough. Told she would know the end is near when she goes blind, she brightly waves Brent off to work, then calmly turns to her friend, Geraldine Fitzgerald, and asks to be led back into the house. It's a moment brain tumor fans often bring up when they talk about the character-building qualities of brain tumors. Before Davis knew of her brain tumor, she was a spoiled socialite. Afterward, she was a model wife. With the possible exception of Woody Allen, actors who learn they have brain tumors tend to act like that.

Stairway to Heaven (1946). Followers of brain tumor scenes consider this memorable and very original film to be the granddaddy of all brain tumor movies. It stars David Niven as a World War II British pilot who jumps from his damaged plane without a parachute and survives. For instance, Niven's only injury, other than having fallen love with Kim Hunter, is a brain tumor. The symptoms of his brain tumor are unique indeed. For instance, Niven smells fried onions before each visit by an eighteenth-century French courtier (Marius Goring), who can freeze people in time while he and Niven have their talks. Goring explains to Niven that since he was supposed to die in the fall, Heaven wants him back. But because Niven has fallen in love during the time he was supposed to be dead, he will be allowed to appeal. Niven's doctor, played marvelously by Roger Livesey, thinks Niven is imagining all this because of his brain tumor.

Livesey dies in a motorcycle accident the night he is supposed to operate on Niven. Instead of becoming Niven's brain surgeon, he becomes Niven's brainy lawyer, and they all go up that wonderful staircase which literally goes to you know where. The stern Raymond Massey, the first American patriot killed in the Revolutionary War, then appears as the prosecutor. It is a particularly nice touch that the trial takes place during the operation. Niven wins his case, pulls through the operation, comes back down the staircase and is allowed to live out his full life span with Kim Hunter. A remarkable film, one that brain tumor fans admit to enjoying on levels that have nothing to do with the genre.

BRIEFCASE

Valkyrie (2008). Though best known as the Tom Cruise eye-patch movie, it is lesser known as the briefcase movie that attempts to blow up Adolf Hitler. It would have worked, too, if the briefcase hadn't been moved farther away from its target. That the camera tracks the briefcase on the day of the attempted assassination rather than sticking with Cruise underscores just how important briefcases can be when they are handled by a director with the right briefcase sensibility.

Iron Man 2 (2010). Probably the most ingenious briefcase scene in movie history involves Robert Downey, Jr. When he opens the briefcase that is thrown to him from a car window, it morphs into a full suit of armor. The scene shows once and for all that it is possible to make body armor portable. In the film series, Downey has also used his high-tech briefcase as a computer.

From Russia with Love (1963). The briefcase in this best of the James Bond films contains a tiny throwing knife, a folding AR-7 rifle, a bottle of talcum powder that is actually tear gas, ammunition in the sides, and 50 gold sovereigns. When it comes to gadgets, Q-branch doesn't fool around. Open the briefcase the wrong way and the tear gas bomb explodes. That's what happens when the Spectre hit man (Robert Shaw) opens it to get the 50 gold sovereigns that Bond tells him is inside, setting off the tear gas and resulting in one of the greatest train compartment fights of all time.

Pulp Fiction (1994). The briefcase in this film of violence and redemption really gets around. It's first spotted in the apartment of the three unlucky guys who stole it from Marcellus. After they get killed, and the delivery boy gets killed, the briefcase is later spotted in a diner, where an unlucky holdup pair nearly get killed trying to steal it. The question of what was in that briefcase is still being discussed by the more anal briefcase scene fans. I haven't watched the scene in a while but I seem to remember it was stuffed with money. I am alone here. All that my briefcase scene brethren remember about the scene is that whatever was in it glowed when Samuel L. Jackson opened it and that Tim Roth went bug-eyed.

Fargo (1996). If you happen to be driving near Fargo, North Dakota, and you spot a crowd of people searching the ground along a barb-wire-fence, there's a reason for this. Somewhere along that fence is where Steve Buscemi buried the briefcase that contained $1 million in ransom. There are two reasons why Buscemi was never able to find it:

    1. It snowed the night after he marked the spot where he buried the briefcase and his marker, along with the entire fence, was buried in the snow.

    2. Buscemi was killed and stuffed into a chopper/mulcher by his fellow kidnapper (Peter Stormire), one of the most frightening kidnappers ever to grace the silver screen.

Mission: Impossible — Ghost Protocol (2011). Tom Cruise has been voted the most unselfish actor in briefcase movie history. This time he plays second banana to a briefcase that everyone wants to get their hands on. The briefcase in question turns out to contain Russian nuclear launch codes that are coveted by brilliant madman Michael Nyqvist, who wants to blow up the world.

BUS STOP

Remains of the Day (1993). Still unable to express his feelings for Emma Thompson as they wait for the bus in the rain, all Anthony Hopkins can manage when Thompson climbs aboard is to raise his hat. Some members of the bus stop fan club theorize that Hopkins's role as Hannibal Lector in *Silence of the Lambs* two years earlier helped him to get a handle on a character who is unable to demonstrate any feeling.

The Laughing Policeman (1973). This is one bus stop the bus should never have stopped at because the passenger who gets on takes out a gun and shoots all the passengers who are already seated. Fan club members never find out why because when the scene is over, they leave the theater.

Forrest Gump (1994). Bus stop movie nuts could have chosen the scene where Tom Hanks is waiting at that bus stop and tells whoever sits next to him, "Life is like a box of chocolates. You never know what you're gonna get." It's a nice, if eccentric, philosophy and Hanks turns his bench at the bus stop into a platform for telling people his life story. But the bus stop scene the membership chose is the final scene in the film, in which Hanks has just put his son on the school bus and sits back down after it leaves. The audience knows that he's going to wait there all day until the bus and his son return. Followers of bus stop scenes in movies agree that when it comes to impact, this one will never be equaled.

Ghost World (2001). Proof that even an unused bus stop can play an important and dramatic role is found in the surreal scenes in this film that are set at one. All through the film an old guy named Norman sits there waiting for a bus that never comes. When it finally does arrive and picks Norman up, Thora Birch feels she has lost her only friend. So the next day, Birch, who has dreamed of running away from home, goes to the bus stop. The bus arrives, she gets on and the film ends with a shot of the bus driving away. Bus stop movie nuts often use this scene to illustrate the restorative powers of bus stops.

BUSINESS CARD

American Psycho (2000). To get through the door of the Best Business Card Scene Fan Club, you have to wear a tie. This is not a problem for business card fans because they wear ties every day. Suits, too. Once through the door, each member must deposit their business card onto a table at the door. The chief executive officer of the club picks each card up and says, "New card? Interesting color." The club member who dropped the card then smiles with satisfaction and says, "That's bone. The lettering is Tillian Grail."

The next arrival takes out his card case, opens it and places his business card on the table. He waits a beat, then says, "Eggshell. With Romalian type. What do you think?"

"Impressive," says the chief executive officer.

A third card is placed on the table. "Raised letters, Polynimbus white."

One of the members says, "Oh my God! You can even see the watermark."

And so it goes until all the members are present. To business card movie nuts, the business card scene in *American Psycho* is without doubt the most satisfying scene in the movie. It has been voted the best business card scene in film history every year since the movie was released.

It should be mentioned that the business card ritual from *American Psycho* cannot end until someone says to the member impersonating Christian Bale, "Something wrong, Patrick? You're sweating." The meetings always end when a waiter brings the check and all the members present place their credit cards over it.

Lost in Translation (2003). Though members of the business card scene fan club prefer scenes in which the protagonist hands out business cards, they grudgingly granted the award to Bill Murray, who, on arriving at a grand hotel in Tokyo, is greeted with not one but five business cards and a fax from his wife telling him he forgot his son's birthday. One of the few members of the club who watched the entire film is reported to have tipped off a friend in the elevator scene fan club that whenever Murray enters an elevator in this movie, he is the tallest one in it.

In accordance with the by-laws of the D.O.A., the Best Business Card Scene in Film History Fan Club, not having supplied the requisite number of scenes in its category, voted to exercise its option to come up with a recipe as a substitution.

ROASTED PEPPERS–ARBUTNEY
(*Three Strangers*, 1946)

Though much better known for his Kaspar Gutman role in *The Maltese Falcon*, Sydney Greenstreet's portrayal of sleazy lawyer Jerome K. Arbutney in *Three Strangers* is Greenstreet at his best. So, what would a lawyer facing disgrace and financial ruin eat after the rich widow (Rosalind Ivan) turned down his proposal of marriage? He made this little snack for himself.

INGREDIENTS
3 or 4 red or yellow bell peppers
4 cloves of garlic
Olive oil
Salt

Greenstreet took the peppers and sliced them into strips, removing the seeds and white veins that line the walls of each pepper. Then he placed the peppers in a cast-iron frying pan, crushing the garlic cloves and placing them in the pan with the peppers. He sprinkled the peppers lightly with salt, covering them with 2 tablespoons of olive oil. Then he placed the peppers underneath a broiler for ten minutes. This done, Greenstreet (as Arbutney) removed the pan from the broiler, stirred the peppers so any charred areas were turned away from the flame and put them back for another 10 minutes. (Yield, if you are not Sydney Greenstreet, two servings.) After removing from the broiler, he let them sit for 10 minutes while he had a strong whiskey and soda. Greenstreet then served this dish to himself with a nice loaf of bread and a sharp cheese. The leftovers were used as a garnish for the chicken sandwich he took to work the next day.

From *Cinema Paradiso*: Laurie Beaufort, the daughter of Eileen O'Hare Beaufort and Gerald Beaufort of Oxnard, Calif. Was married Friday to Bruce

Arbuthnot, the son of Rose Lois Arbuthnot and Dr. Theodore Arbutnot of New York City. The bride, 31, a graduate of Princeton University, is a second-year member of the Best Brain Tumor Fan Club. Her favorite film is *Dark Victory* (1939) because Bette Davis's symptoms (inability to concentrate on her bridge game and double vision when the horse she is riding is about to jump a fence) show that the rich have better brain tumor symptoms than the rest of us. The groom, 26, a graduate of NYU, is a fourth-year member of the Best Laughing Scene Fan Club. His favorite movie is *Sometimes a Great Notion* (1971), in which Richard Jaeckel became the only actor in movie history to drown laughing. The ceremony, officiated by Blaise Hospodar, a distant relative of Edmond O'Brien and a specially ordained member of the D.O.A., was held on a Friday night, the traditional movie night for dating couples. Marriage proposal fans in attendance were pleased to learn that the groom used the same phrase in his proposal to the bride that Paul Lukas used when he proposed to Katharine Hepburn in *Little Women* (1937). The phrase he began his marriage proposal with, "dare I hope," has never before or since been used in movies.

BUTTON

The Private Affairs of Bel Ami (1947). Most button scene enthusiasts consider this nearly forgotten film to contain not one but two of the best button scenes in film history. When Katherine Emory, at George Sanders's knee, begins to wind her hair around one of his jacket buttons, the excitement can be felt from every button scene fan in the audience. Heightening the effect is the lack of attention Sanders pays to her or what she is doing. When Sanders suddenly gets up from the chair, taking a strand of her hair with him, button scene fans have been known to literally jump from their seats. An especially nice touch is how the camera lingers on Emory's face to show the exquisite pain and pleasure Sanders's button caused her. The knowledge that this strand of hair leads to another button scene keeps the attention of fans riveted on the button with the strand of hair wound around it. There it remains until Angela Lansbury spots the strand of hair on Sanders's button and utters the line everyone has been waiting for: "Oh, look, someone has wound their hair around one of your buttons." Lansbury's words have recently been immortalized in a needlepoint sampler that now hangs in the Button Scene Hall of Fame.

Father of the Bride (1950). Isn't it odd how buttons bring out the worst in wives? Joan Bennett is the sweetest of women all through this delightful comedy of manners, but when faced with a button scene, she suddenly develops a sharp tongue. It happens while Spencer Tracy is trying on his old cutaway. Tracy, who hasn't worn his tails in twenty years, does a boffo job of proving he can still fit into them by managing to button every button of his very tight vest. He tops this off with the jacket, which he can barely get his arms into. Tracy manages to button its single button only after finding a posture that makes him look like a cross between Dr. Frankenstein's hunchback servant and Walter Matthau.

So what is Bennett's reaction to all this when Tracy calls her in to view the result of his efforts? She takes one look at the button on Tracy's jacket and delivers what must be one of the meanest button lines in recent screen memory: "If that button gets away, it's going to put out someone's eye!"

The Big Chill (1985). Merely the rumor that this scene was being considered for an award gave button scene enthusiasts a reputation for being morbid. True, the scene takes place in a funeral home, and yes, the object being buttoned is a corpse, and yes again, the mortician seems to be wearing red nail polish. To explain all this, button scene fans prefer to go over each point individually. First, they are always on the lookout for unusual button scene locales and what is more unusual than a button scene in a funeral home? Second, what else would be buttoned in a funeral home but the clothes on a corpse? Finally, they resent any untoward suggestions deriving from the fact that they like a scene in which a mortician wears red nail polish, pointing out the obvious — the mortician is a woman.

CAR CHASE

Bullitt (1968). At the opening of the monthly meeting of the car chase scene fan club, the chancellor raps his gavel and asks the members, "Why are there hills in San Francisco?"

"So there can be great car chase scenes!" the members roar back.

The basis for this ritual is the classic car chase in this taut thriller. When Steve McQueen suddenly guns his sports car around the block and winds up tailing the killers who are tailing him, car chase fans can feel their antennae go up. When the driver of the car McQueen is tailing spots him in the rearview mirror and buckles his seat belt, and the killer beside him does the same, car chase fans take out their portable seat belts and buckle up, too. (No true car chase fan ever goes to see this film without one.)

The actual chase is not only wonderfully orchestrated and photographed, but it also develops a definite rhythm each time one of the cars reaches the crest of a hill, leaves the ground and thumps back to earth. The chase picks up even more speed and tension as it makes its way out onto the freeway, where McQueen has to submit to a shotgun blast before the killers meet their fiery end by ramming into a gas truck.

One group of car chase mathematicians has been trying to work out how many minutes the chase was on screen, but they are unable to agree on when the chase actually begins. A second group has been attempting to work out how many miles were covered in the chase and whether one or both cars should have run out of gas. That both reports are many years overdue does not diminish the brilliance of this chase, which to date has not been topped.

The French Connection (1971). Probably the least desirable place in the world to shoot a car chase is New York City. But a car chasing a subway train is another matter altogether. For this type of chase to work, the subway has to be above ground. No problem. New York City has plenty of those. Also, Gene Hackman has to commandeer a car. No problem. Hackman steps in front of a speeding car and gets the driver to give it to him by saying, "Police emergency. I need your car." Even usually serious car chase fans never fail to be amused when the driver asks Hackman (who has already begun to speed away), "Hey, when am I going to get it back?" Better he should never have asked.

Chasing a subway train speeding 30 feet over your head involves a lot of looking up. Hackman rams the poor fellow's car into a truck, another car, and a few steel girders, and also nearly hits a mother pushing a baby carriage. But he keeps up with the train and pays back the drug smuggler who tried to snuff him out by killing him. To those who think subway trains are easy to follow because they can't leave the tracks, car chase scene fans simply repeat what Hackman says when asked the same question: "Try chasing one!"

Foul Play (1978). When Gilbert and Sullivan wrote *The Mikado* in 1885, neither one had a car chase in mind. But don't tell that to car chase fans who consider the music for this operetta to be the perfect background score for one. The car chase in the film is a witty parody of the one in *Bullitt*. It, too, takes place in San Francisco. The action begins when Chevy Chase and Goldie

Hawn commandeer a limousine so they can get to the opera to prevent the assassination of the pope, who is seeing *The Mikado.*

To a car chase fan, the reasons for the chase don't matter; it just has to be a good ride. This one is, with all the necessary ingredients — intersection running, sidewalk hopping, sudden turns and fender bending — that one would expect. There's even an unexpected bonus in the form of an elderly Japanese couple in the rear of the limousine who do not speak English. They huddle in the back, not knowing what is happening until Chase tries to tell them he is a policeman and Hawn mentions "Kojak." This they understand and enjoy the rest of the ride, a nice touch and one that garnered the scene enough votes to put it on the list.

It's a Mad, Mad, Mad, Mad World (1963). When asked what movie contains a car chase that has cars, trucks, planes, fireworks, and a mother-in-law; lasts for the entire movie; and is carefully mapped and followed by a long-suffering policeman who is trying to settle a domestic dispute between his wife and daughter, very few film fans would fail to name this movie. Car chase fans feel no other reason for their selection is necessary and rest their case.

CARD

The Cincinnati Kid (1965). A card scene fan following Steve McQueen's poker odyssey along the three river towns might feel like a kid in a candy store. There are so many memorable card games that choosing the best one is as difficult as trying to fill an inside straight. The one ultimately chosen is a poker hand early in the film. Rip Torn and Edward G. Robinson are playing a game of five-card stud, head to head. McQueen, the main character, isn't even present. The last card has just been dealt. Torn bets $2,000. He shows no pair and no picture card. Robinson, who also shows no pair and no picture card, calls and raises $2,000. Torn calls the raise. He has jack high, no pair. Robinson wins the hand with queen high, no pair. Not a particularly masterfully played hand, but one that won card scene fans over because of Robinson's devastating reply to Torn when he asks how Robinson knew he only had a jack as his hole card. "Son," Robinson says, "all you pay is the looking price. Lessons are extra."

The Odd Couple (1968). No collection of great card scenes could ever be complete without a weekly card game and no one knows how to capture the feel of a weekly game better than Neil Simon. Simon doesn't even make us wait long; he comes across with one in the opening scene of this very funny film. It has the right amount of card players, the right amount of smoke and the right amount of six-week-old potato chips.

From the moment Vinnie (the winner who always has to be home by twelve) asks what time it is and is told, "You're winning $95, that's what time it is," card scene fans know they are in the hands of someone who probably hasn't missed his Thursday night poker game in 15 years. Walter Matthau's eloquent rationale for why he plays poker touched the heart of every card scene fan present at the final vote. Matthau explains that he plays cards because he needs the money. He always loses. Which is why he needs the money.

Captain Horatio Hornblower (1951). Though few card scene fans know how to play whist, many know a great whist scene when they see one. This is a great one and Gregory Peck's portrayal of an English sea captain with a passion for cards is flawless. When he invites his officers to his quarters for a rubber of whist, not knowing whether the enemy Spanish ship *Natividad* will sail around the point or snug down for the night, card game fans are ashiver with anticipation. If the *Natividad* snugs down for the night, they know they will see a rubber of whist completed. If it spots Peck's ship, they will see whist players blown out of the water doing what they love best — playing whist. As the *Natividad* makes its final tack, Peck even takes the time to lecture one of his officers on the correct card to play. The fact that Peck risks his life and those of his men in betting the Spanish ship will snug down so he can finish the rubber adds much to the tension and eventual pleasure of this scene. The scene is also proof that the Napoleonic War of 1812 could produce a first-class game of cards.

Born Yesterday (1950). Gin players among the card scene fan membership insist that Judy Holliday won her Academy Award for the masterful way she beats Broderick Crawford in their now classic gin game. Crawford, wearing a tuxedo, should have learned not to yell "Do you mind!" at Holliday when she sings while she plays because the next card she picks up is always her gin card.

The Foxes of Harrow (1947). Card scene fans who have been waiting for someone to cry, "Innkeeper, pen and pencil," at a dramatic point in a game of cards are rewarded in this scene in which Rex Harrison wins a plantation from Hugo Haas, a loudmouthed card player with a German accent. That alone would be enough to put it in the awards category, but there is more. We are treated to a streak of card player luck that is rare in films. Harrison sits down to a game of *Chemin de fer* as a pauper, with nothing more than his lucky tie pin, and gets up a member of the landowner gentry. If that isn't enough to fill an inside straight, we also get to see the loudmouthed card player turn out to be a poor loser, insult the woman Harrison loves, and get killed in a duel. The game is so superbly orchestrated, and Haas is enough of a boor, that few film fans mind when he gets shot.

It would be hard to list all the actors who looked as if they were born holding a deck of cards, but three perennial favorites are Frank Sinatra, for bluffing Dean Martin out of pot in *Some Came Running* (1959); Dean Martin in the same film, for taking it with such good grace, and Paul Newman, for bluffing a fellow chain-gang prisoner in *Cool Hand Luke* (1967) and out-cheating Robert Shaw in that high-stakes game on the train in *The Sting* (1973).

CAT

The Wrong Box (1967). When Peter Sellers used a kitten as a blotter in his role as the seedy Dr. Pratt, a roar of disapproval went up from cat lovers. Cat scene lovers, however, fell off their seats laughing and voted it as one of the best cat scenes in film history. The same opposite reactions occurred when Peter Cook accidently sat on one of the many cats in Sellers's office. One needn't be a great genius to see that a cat lover is not necessarily a cat scene lover, nor a cat scene lover a cat lover. Perhaps it was to appease the former group that Sellers informed the kitten he had used as a blotter, "I was not always as you see me now."

The Incredible Shrinking Man (1957). In this film about cat revenge, cats got even for one of their own getting sprayed with paint in *The Invisible Man* (1933). Cat lovers, however, were not mollified. They felt that the film portrayed cats as ungrateful animals who will eat their masters the moment they shrink, citing the scene in which the cat tried to do just that after discovering that her master had dropped to the size of a mouse and was living in his daughter's dollhouse. Cat scene lovers would not comment on this, but were reported to be amused when a group of cat lovers petitioned the government to make dollhouses cat-proof.

The Third Man (1950). A cat is the first to know that Harry Lime (Orson Welles) is alive. When it scoots out of Valli's apartment and down the deserted Vienna street, cat scene fans in the audience have a hard time restraining themselves from egging it on. By the time the cat stops at a doorway and begins to lick someone's well-shined shoes, everyone in the audience knows that Harry Lime isn't dead. It's not that difficult to figure out, since we already know that Harry Lime is the only person the cat likes. A shaft of light from the window, a zither crescendo, and Welles's insolent smile when the light hits his face all top off a cat scene worth remembering.

The Invisible Man (1933). Another scene that cat scene lovers adore and cat lovers don't occurs in this film starring Claude Rains in the title role. The award-winning scene comes toward the end of the film while the police are protecting Dr. Kemp from Rains. Kemp is Rains's former assistant and Rains has promised to kill him for calling the police on him. To make sure they can detect the invisible Rains, the police first put earth on top of the wall surrounding the house. That way they will see the earth move if Rains attempts to climb over. Then they arm themselves with spritzers filled with paint. The idea is that if Rains does get on the grounds, one spritz and they'll see him. However, the plan backfires when a cat leaps onto the wall. A clump of dirt falls on one of the policemen, who then sprays the poor cat full of paint. The spritzer plan may not have caught Rains, but it did result in a memorable cat scene.

Cinderella (1950). Cat lovers again cried foul. Lucifer, Walt Disney's cat villain in this animated fairy tale, would certainly have stopped Jacques and Gus (Cinderella's two mice friends) from delivering the key to her had it not been for Bruno, the dog. To cat scene lovers, it didn't matter a bit that the key allowed Cinderella to unlock the door, try on the glass slipper and marry the Prince. Nowhere in the *Cat Scene Manual* does it say that great cat performances need to be burdened with plot considerations or that cats have to be treated with kid gloves. Cat lovers, on the other hand, felt that it was grossly unfair for Disney to bring in a dog to stop Lucifer from keeping Cinderella from being rescued by the two mice.

So high did feelings run among the cat lover clique in the cat scene fan clubhouse that they vowed to get even. They made good on that vow six years later: the two Siamese cats in Disney's *Lady and the Tramp* (1955) were denied an award they justly deserved and were consigned to cat scene oblivion.

Actors who have shown a particular sensitivity to cats include the incomparable Charles Grey and all the other actors who played Ernst Stavros Blofield, the head of S.P.E.C.T.R.E., in all the James Bond films. Kim Novak is also popular with cat scene lovers for the way she used her cat, Piwacket, to cast a spell on Jimmy Stewart in *Bell, Book, and Candle* (1958). What cat scene lovers don't like is that Novak loses Piwacket's affections because she falls in love with Stewart. And let's not forget Art Carney, who takes his cat Tonto on a cross-country roadtrip in *Harry and Tonto* (1974).

CEMETERY

Mr. Hulot's Holiday (1953). Not even a cemetery could restrain the irrepressible Jacques Tati. In cemetery scene circles, the scene he created in this French import is considered a masterpiece of timing and wit. To work as it did, three crucial elements had to fall into place: Tati's spare tire had to roll into the wet leaves; he had to pick it up at the exact moment a funeral party arrived at the cemetery; and the funeral party had to mistake the leaf-covered tire for a wreath and Tati for a mourner. The rest was easy. Tati was too sweet-natured to refuse their invitation to join them at the graveside and too polite to tell them not to nail his spare tire into the tree.

One group of cemetery scene fans were so taken with this scene they plan to travel to Jacques. Tati's gravesite to re-create it. Other than finding an automobile tire thin enough to be mistaken for a funeral wreath when covered with wet leaves, they foresee no difficulty.

The Third Man (1950). Cemetery scene fans have a special fondness for movies in which the final scene is set in a cemetery. So when Joseph Cotten gets out of Trevor Howard's car to wait for Alida Valli outside that Viennese cemetery, they are all rooting for her to forgive him for shooting Harry Lime. As she walks toward Cotten, the zither crescendo gives them reason to believe she will. But Valli walks past him. Worse, she doesn't even look at him. One of the great movie endings, but romantically disappointing. It should be noted that cemetery scene fans find the rumor that Valli could forgive Cotten for killing Lime, but not for getting Doctor Vinkle's name wrong, to be in very bad taste.

The African Queen (1951). Perhaps the quickest and least sentimental funeral in film history is the one given to Robert Morley, who didn't quite make it through the first fifteen minutes of the movie alive. Humphrey Bogart's explanation of the hasty burial is also lacking in tender feelings. He tells Katharine Hepburn (Morley's sister), "What with the climate and all, the quicker we get him in the ground, the better." Sentimentality aside, cemetery scene fans have a particular warm spot for this very brief funeral because cemetery scenes shot in Africa are rare. Best line: Bogart's delicately phrased response when Hepburn tells him that her brother is dead — "Aw, ain't that awful."

The Wrong Box (1969). For cemetery scene fans whose taste for funerals runs to undertakers in top hats draped with crepe, this English import has two sets of undertakers in top hats draped with crepe. For those who enjoy a high-speed chase with horse-drawn hearses, a switch of caskets, and a knockdown brawl between the two "corpses," this very funny film obliges once again. Add to all this a game cast that refused to be buffaloed into solemnity at funerals—Dudley Moore, Fred Cook, Ralph Richardson, John Mills, and Michael Caine, to name a few—and one has what one cemetery scene fan (who rates them the old-fashioned way) calls a four-star cemetery scene.

The Good, the Bad and the Ugly (1966). Cemetery scene delicacy is not one of Clint Eastwood's strong points. In the final cemetery scene of this Sergio Leone release, he shoots Lee Van Cleef and strings up Eli Wallach so that he has to balance on a wooden grave marker or hang. Then Eastwood rides off to leave him. When Wallach protests, Eastwood, in what must be the best feat of cemetery scene marksmanship in screen history, casually takes out his rifle and shoots down the rope. In a separate ballot, fans voted this the best cemetery scene in a spaghetti western, which to some movie fans is like being voted the best second baseman in Bulgaria.

Freud (1962). With the selection of this now almost forgotten John Huston film about a Viennese cemetery's contribution to psychiatry, cemetery scene fans seem to be saying that cemeteries are not a good place to resolve an Oedipus complex. Montgomery Clift found this to be true when Freud, the character he portrayed, fainted at the cemetery gates during a visit to his father's grave. For Freud, it was a breakthrough—the formulation of one of his most important theories. For cemetery scene fans, it was simply a good cemetery scene, better than most and certainly deserving of this mention.

Frankenstein (1931). A cemetery scene collection without a Frankenstein film would be like a werewolf movie without a full moon. Cemetery scene fans may have placed this one last on their list in order to cap their category off with a classic, but James Whale, the film's director, opened with it. This is a cemetery scene with all the necessary ingredients: fog and a gravedigger with the right touch of nonchalance. This plays wonderfully against the tension of Colin Clive (Herr Frankenstein) and his servant Fritz, who wait behind the gate for the gravedigger to finish filling in the grave. An especially nice touch is the exaggerated sound of the earth hitting the casket. Cemetery scene sound experts report that this may be the loudest instance of earth hitting a wooden casket in film history. Best moment: As Clive and Fritz are digging up the casket, Clive sort of hugs it, exclaiming with great excitement, "He's just resting, waiting for a new life to come!"

Western cemetery scene fans felt a special honor should go to Ward Bond. Bond, who could sing "Shall We Gather at the River" with the best of them, was paid this mark of respect for finding time to attend nearly every western funeral ever filmed.

CHRISTMAS CARD

Diary of a Mad Housewife (1970). Probably the most selfish and unlikeable husband in film history is Richard Benjamin. The scene where he is putting up the Christmas cards in the library of his Central Park West apartment is a small gem. While up on a ladder arranging the cards, Benjamin turns to his long-suffering wife, Carrie Snodgrass, and tells her they've done really well this year. We sent out 254 cards and received 387. No wonder Snodgrass has an affair with Frank Langella. But he turns out to be a selfish putz as well. Langella is so bad that one of the women he treats badly tells him she's going to report him to Women's Lib.

Understanding that Christmas cards do not make for a lot of dramatic scenes, the club has created a Christmas drink for men who treat women badly. They've called it a *Putzkiller.*

INGREDIENTS

2 jiggers whiskey
1 jigger gin
1 jigger Pernod

Place ice cubes in a shaker, then add all the ingredients and shake well. Strain into a martini glass.

Author's note: Not for the occasional putz.

Love Actually (2003). It wasn't until 33 years after Richard Benjamin counted the Christmas cards he received that Christmas card aficionados found another scene worthy of mention. There is not one word of dialogue in the entire scene, which helps make it special. On Christmas Eve, Andrew Lincoln appears at Keira Knightley's door with a boom box that plays "Silent Night" and a stack of hand-printed cards that tell her he will always love her. That to him she is perfect. And that his wasted heart will love her until she looks like this (that card has a photograph of a 5,000-year-old pretty well-preserved mummy). The last card says Merry Christmas. The only problem is that Knightley just got married to Lincoln's best friend. But the Christmas cards get him a nice kiss from Knightley before he leaves her forever.

CIGAR

Lifeboat (1944). This film has earned its place on the list if only for the extraordinary length of time a cigar is seen on camera. The manner in which

Henry Hull nurses his solitary Bolivar Corona Gigante through storm, poker game, drought, and, finally, the murder of Walter Slezak, is a lesson in platonic cigar love from which many cigar smokers could benefit. It is only natural that a film in which cigar lifeboat etiquette is raised to such heights should be the one that superficially appears to violate Rule 5 in the *Cigar Scene Manual*, which refers to the unimportance of cigar scene length. Most dramatic scene: Not the sly manner in which Walter Slezak causes the watery demise of William Bendix, but Hull's unfortunate discovery that the box of Havanas he has rescued from the sinking ship contains only one cigar.

A Dangerous Method (2011). Topping Henry Hull as the actor who gives a cigar the longest screen time in film history is Viggo Mortensen. His portrayal of Sigmund Freud was so cigar accurate that even when he fainted and fell to the floor, the cigar he was smoking stayed between his lips. For this trick, Mortensen was awarded a Kipling, a rarely given honor named after English writer, Rudyard Kipling, whose poem "Betrothed" compares the virtues of cigars to those of women.

P.J. (1968). To a cigar scene fan, Raymond Burr will forever be the granddaddy of cigar misers. With an entire humidor filled with expensive Cuban cigars, Burr kept a special section for butts. Though Arnold Zellermeyer reports that he was privately shocked at the sight of all those half-smoked Havanas, he confesses that it was the look in Burr's eyes as he fondled his cigar-butt treasure that won this scene a place on the awards list and exonerated him of the murder of the beautiful Gayle Hunnicut.

Miller's Crossing (1990). After 44 years, the search committee for the best cigar scenes in film history found a cigar miser to equal Raymond Burr. Forget the special cigar butt section Burr kept in his humidor — Albert Finney, an Irish gangster, does him one better. While lying in bed smoking a cigar and listening to a recording of "Danny Boy," he sees smoke coming through the floor boards and hears footsteps. He calmly tamps out his cigar and puts it in his silk bathrobe. Then he reaches for the gun on the night table. Hiding under the bed, he shoots one of the gangsters who have come to kill him and jumps out the window. Finney calmly waits for the other gangster and plugs him, too. All this barely registers on cigar scene movie nuts, who keep staring at Finney's bathrobe pocket. Then, when a car pulls up and starts shooting at Finney with a tommy gun, he calmly picks up one of the tommy guns of the dead gangster and fires back at the car until it crashes into a tree and bursts into flames. It is then, but only then, that Finney reaches into his pocket to retrieve his cigar butt and calmly lights it. If you happen to be passing the cigar scene clubhouse on Madison Avenue and 51st Street and hear cries of "bravo," this is the moment that the membership are watching.

Witness for the Prosecution (1958). Who but the most phlegmatic of cigar smokers would fail to feel a frisson of terror watching Elsa Lanchester trying to ferret out Charles Laughton's hidden cigar. Laughton's ingenious ability to keep his cigar lit in the face of Lanchester's determination to deny him this pleasure has won him his well-deserved Kipling. Laughton's deft cigar frisk of the solicitor and his willingness to listen to the boring details of the case are the main charms of this film.

One cigar scene enthusiast reports that he learned the trick of keeping his cigar-hating third wife ignorant of his cigar habit from Laughton's clever technique of always having a third party present whenever he wished to enjoy a cigar. When discovered, one can always rely on the visitor to claim owner-ship. Film historians may be interested to learn that Laughton was the first actor to use a cigar "beard" on screen.

Citizen Kane (1941). This classic film actually contains two memorable cigar scenes and Joseph Cotten, among all the great cigar-smoking actors in Hollywood, is the only one to pull off a "double claro," winning two Kiplings for a single performance. The first award is for his sensitive relighting of his Partagas Lusitania after Welles discovers him drunk over his typewriter. There were some in the selection committee who felt this first Kipling was a senti-mental choice. After all, wasn't he fired by Welles after he relights it? And wasn't it his love of cigars that kept him a bachelor during the film?

Cotten's second Kipling was more unanimous. His portrayal of an old man yearning for a cigar has yet to be equaled on the silver screen. He literally has cigar scene fans at the edge of their seats when he tries to enlist a young reporter to sneak a "see-gar" into his old-age home. "You don't happen to have a good see-gar on you?" he asks. "I have a young physician who thinks I shouldn't smoke." Thrilling words, topped only by Cotten's final plea: "You won't forget those see-gars, will you? Make 'em look like toothpaste or something." If there is a more moving moment in cigar film history, I haven't seen it.

The only flaw in the film is that Welles, a cigar smoker himself, never allows us to see if the young reporter kept his promise.

Notorious (1946). Cigars don't have to be seen to make it a great cigar scene. Toward the end of this classic film, Ingrid Bergman tells Claude Rains, who plays the wealthy villain, that she will be going into town. Rains replies, "Will you see if my cigars have arrived? There should be about a thousand of them. If they have, ask them to keep them in the humidor for me." But when cigars are seen on the screen, they have to be good. Not the cheap tiparello with a plastic tip that Lt. Dan smokes in *Forrest Gump* (1994). Ditto for those two-bit cigars Clint Eastwood smokes in *The Good, the Bad and the Ugly* (1966).

Dr. Strangelove (1964). The cigar that Sterling Hayden (as Gen. Jack Ripper) smokes in this scene while explaining to Peter Sellers how he denies his precious bodily fluids has not yet been identified, but all club members agree that it must have been a good one. Nobody who is about to blow his head off in the bathroom smokes a cheap cigar. Cigar scene aficionados have had better luck with the cigar Gene Hackman smokes in *Crimson Tide* (1995). It is a Montecristo #2.

Bride of Frankenstein (1935). James Whale was surely a cigar smoker. Why else would he include a scene in which the blind hermit (O.P. Heggie) teaches Frankenstein's monster (Boris Karloff) how to smoke? As Karloff says when he takes his first puff of the cigar, "Good. Cigar good!"

The Maltese Falcon (1941). Many admirers of this classic cigar whodunit hold the mistaken notion that Sydney Greenstreet doctored Humphrey Bogart's drink so Elisha Cook would have an easier time of kicking him in the ribs when he blacked out. This was not the case. New evidence from Greenstreet's secret cigar diary supports Zellermeyer's long-held theory that Bogart actually fainted with pleasure from the H. Upmann Double Corona offered him by the Fat Man.

Greenstreet's cigar persona is so profound that many of his fans are still not certain whether he was smoking one when he proposed to Lady Belladon in *Three Strangers* (1946).

Charlie Bubbles (1968). Cigar scene fans especially like this film, if only for the infinite variety of places in which Albert Finney smokes a cigar. Finney smokes what have been definitively identified as Montecristo #1's while getting crème brûlée pushed into his face; while getting drunk in a pool hall; while watching a soccer game; while watching television monitors in his Georgian home; while driving his Rolls Royce; and, in what is Zellermeyer's favorite scene, while drying Colin Blakely's trousers in the men's room at Hyde Park.

There are many other fine actors who know their way around a fine cigar, and no piece on the pleasures of cigar scenes would be complete without giving them a mention. The list is only partial, but it is dedicated to all screen actors who have shown the proper cigar delicacy in their roles: Charles Coburn, for the Rey Del Mondo Lonesdales he smoked in *The Paradine Case* (1948); John Huston, for his masterful portrayal of a cigar-smoking cardinal in *The Cardinal* (1963); Lee J. Cobb, for *On the Waterfront* (1954); Edward G. Robinson, for smoking one in the bathtub in *Key Largo* (1948); Eugene Palette for the patient manner in which he smoked his Montecristo #2's in *100 Men and a Girl* (1937); and finally Simon Ward, for his sensitive re-creation of Winston Churchill smoking his first cigar in *Young Winston* (1972).

CIGARETTE CASE

The Private Affairs of Bel Ami (1947). To show George Sanders how much she loves him, Clothilde (Angela Lansbury) secretly measures his cigarette case so she can fit a photograph of herself inside it. During that now famous ride in a coach, she asks him for his cigarette case and places her photo inside it, delivering the line that is so loved by cigarette case fans: "I can measure the dimensions of this cigarette case, but who can measure the dimensions of your heart." Sanders must have realized this would become a classic cigarette case scene, because he responds with an equally immortal line: "I could be happy with you, Clothilde."

A New Leaf (1971). In this very funny film about the value and price of cigarette cases, Walter Matthau is no hero to cigarette case fans. Yes, he gives his cigarette case to his smarmy lawyer to satisfy a $550 debt, but he does so at the very beginning of the movie, making it a certainty that the cigarette case will not be seen again. Even the fact that this is a film starring and directed by Elaine May is not enough to dissuade cigarette case fans from leaving the theater after this scene is over.

Seven Days in May (1964). Had it not been for Edmond O'Brien's cigarette case, Burt Lancaster might have become the first Army general to overthrow the American government. Cigarette case enthusiasts, unused to seeing cigarette case scenes play such an important role in a film, flock in droves to this film about the value of keeping important documents in cigarette cases. The scene they come for is the one in which the Spanish soldier finds O'Brien's cigarette case in the plane wreckage, the same case given to him by the president of the United States. O'Brien had the foresight to put the signed confession he had obtained from an admiral into that very cigarette case. The case, and the evidence needed to foil the plot against the president, survived the crash. Unfortunately, O'Brien, now fully recovered from having been murdered in *D.O.A.*, did not.

Room at the Top (1959). Laurence Harvey doesn't get the chance to use the cigarette case that Simone Signoret gives him for very long in this wonderful New Wave British film. When Signoret's husband finds out about her affair with Harvey, he walks into Harvey's office and takes it back, but not before removing Harvey's cigarettes. "A putz without a heart" was the general feeling among cigarette case scene movie nuts. Simone's Best Actress Oscar was not much compensation.

CLIFF JUMPING

Butch Cassidy and the Sundance Kid (1969). The film was nominated for 7 Oscars and won for best screenplay. Cliff jumping movie nuts like to think a big part of this recognition was due to Paul Newman and Robert Redford's cliff jump. With the posse behind them, and nowhere to go but down, Redford would rather fight than jump into the river below because he can't swim. Newman bursts out laughing and tells Redford he's crazy because the fall will probably kill him anyway. Cliff jumping fans like what Redford says when they jump, which, if you listen hard, sounds a lot like "Oh sh-eeee-t!"

Papillon (1973). If you're ever a prisoner on Devil's Island and you want to escape, Steve McQueen should be your go-to guy. It was McQueen who figured out that it's the seventh wave that will take you out to sea. But you have to jump off the cliff first. Dustin Hoffman didn't want to jump and he has forever been labeled by the club's members as a cliff jump sissy.

Apocalypto (2006). To escape his pursuers, Rudy Youngblood jumps into a raging river from a pretty high cliff. Much to the club members' delight, we get a few more cliff jumps when the leader of the pursuers urges his men to jump off the cliff after Youngblood. Director Mel Gibson orders two of the pursuers to crack their heads open on the submerged river rocks. No cliff jump movie nut can remember ever seeing a cliff jump fatality like this before.

King Kong (1933). Okay, so it isn't technically a cliff jump. Yet lawyers for cliff jump fans persuaded the jury that the jump Fay Wray and Bruce Cabot make from the vine hanging off that cliff qualifies as a cliff jump. When Kong starts to pull the vine up to get Wray back, they both let go and plunge to the water below. In a lighter moment cliff jump aficionados point out that the reason Wray doesn't scream as she is falling is because her voice is shot from all the screaming she did when she first laid eyes on Kong.

Potato peeling movie nuts, who share quarters with cliff jumping scene fans, have long been upset at the paucity of potato peeling scenes in film. Unfortunately, their claim that the best line in this film is when the freighter's Chinese cook says, "Someday I go back to China and never have to peel potatoes," never caught on.

Crouching Tiger, Hidden Dragon (2000). The most beautiful cliff jump in movie history is the one taken by Jen, the governor's daughter and unwitting protégée of the Jade Fox, the oldest master swordswoman still active in film. Jen's lover told her of the legend of a man who jumped off a cliff to make his wishes come true and did not die because his heart was pure. When Jen jumps in the final scene of the movie after her lover makes a wish that they be together forever, she just floats down through the clouds. To a cliff jump aficionado, cliff jumps like this don't get any better.

Author's note: The Twilight movies may have grossed over $144 million, but not with the help of the cliff jumping fan club. No self-respecting cliff jumping movie nut would pay $13 to see one. As a result, Kristen Stewart's cliff jump in The Twilight Saga: New Moon *(2009) was not on the ballot. Jake's cliff jump (or, more accurately, his avatar's cliff jump) in* Avatar *(2009) wasn't nominated in the cliff jump category either because it was computer generated.*

CLOCK

The Stranger (1946). When Orson Welles doesn't like a character he is playing, he certainly knows how to do him in. The beneficiaries of this sentiment are clock scene fans who are treated to what may be the first "clock murder" in film history. Welles, who starred in and directed this film, plays a Nazi with a mania for clocks. It is the final scene, set in the old clock tower, which strikes the fancy of clock scene fans.

By the time this scene rolls around, everyone in the sleepy little college town of Harper knows who Welles really is. Loretta Young, his wife, tries to shoot him. She succeeds, but also shoots the clock mechanism, which sends the knight with a sword and the angel it is chasing both traveling around the belfry at lethal speeds. Wounded, Welles staggers to the ledge outside, where the angel and knight are racing around; he sidesteps the angel, but gets impaled on the knight's sword. Freeing himself, he pushes the knight off the ledge and then, mortally wounded, falls to his death. A very satisfying ending and one that goes into the clock scene record book as the first time a clock ever stabbed an actor.

The last line of this film has always puzzled clock scene fans and made them wonder if Edward G. Robinson, who was responsible for catching Welles, wasn't a bit of a sadist. After telling Loretta Young her husband is a Nazi and watching her shoot him, then seeing him get skewered by a clock and fall 500 feet to his death, he says to her, "Pleasant dreams."

Laura (1944). Although the sudden demise of Clifton Webb's clock has been clearly established as "death by misadventure," clock scene fans still consider it clock murder and cannot forgive Webb for blasting it with his shotgun. Didn't Webb know that when you play with shotguns around clocks, clocks are bound to get hurt? Dana Andrews is also not very popular in clock scene circles. Didn't he know that by shooting Webb while Webb was pointing a shotgun, it was likely to go off? Gene Tierney has a lot to answer for as well. Why wasn't she home when Webb came to murder her?

It is the clock who is the only innocent party in the entire dirty affair. Is there anyone, anywhere, who thinks that it deserved to be blown apart by Webb after allowing Webb to hide the instrument of its death in its inner workings? Oh, it's a great clock scene, all right, but the award was given with a very heavy heart.

Wild Strawberries (1957). Though Ingmar Bergman's films are not in vogue at the moment, the clock scene in this movie about an elderly professor reviewing his life remains timeless. It takes place in a dream sequence when the protagonist is walking though a town and sees a steeple clock with no hands. One needn't be a clock scene fan to know that a clock without hands symbolizes death. Clock scene fans, however, are not the best people to ask if the clock symbol in this Bergman film was accurate, since they always leave after this scene and haven't seen the end of the film yet.

Safety Last (1923). There's a good reason why clock scene movie nuts keep the wall clock in their clubhouse set at precisely 2:45 in the afternoon. Had the hands on the large clock on the Los Angeles office building not been pointing to that time, Harold Lloyd would not have been able to reach out and grab the hands and movie fans would have been deprived of an iconic, nail-biting clock scene. The clock scene clubhouse is not listed in the telephone directory, but a good way to find it is to follow someone wearing a straw hat and horn-rimmed glasses.

Back to the Future (1985). Christopher Lloyd is no Harold Lloyd but as Dr. Emmett Brown he does a pretty neat job in the clock tower scene as he struggles to connect that wire in time for the lightning strike that will power the DeLorean time machine Michael J. Fox is driving and send him back to the future.

Hugo (2011). You gotta love a movie about a 12-year-old boy who lives between the walls of the Gare Montparnasse railway station and takes care of the clocks. The clock has a nice peephole through which the boy can watch the happenings below. Clock fans are particularly taken with the scene where he eludes the station inspector by running to the top of the clock tower and climbing out onto the clock's hands. Since 12-year-olds don't weigh as much as Harold Lloyd, the hands don't break. Martin Scorsese, the film's director, owes a lot to Lloyd and this enchanting film was nominated for a Best Picture and won an Academy Award for Best Cinematography.

COOKING

I Remember Mama (1948) Every writer in the cooking scene fan club wishes they had a mother like Irene Dunne. To get the famed writer Mrs. Moorehead (Florence Bates) to read her daughter's story, she gives Bates her prized recipe for Norwegian meatballs with cream sauce. Moviegoers only hear three details but they are important enough to get the scene on this list: the meat is ground six times, the meatballs are cooked in boiling stock, and the sauce is one-half sour cream. Dunne even surpasses the mother in a very funny New Yorker cartoon who bursts into an editor's office holding a manuscript. The caption: *"You didn't like my son's book?"*

Babette's Feast (1987). Don't go to see this film if you're hungry. We not only see the meal being eaten but we also see Stephane Audran cooking it. The courses include turtle soup, Blinis Demidoff with caviar, and cailles en sarcophages (quails in coffins). When the Danish general (Jarl Kulle) tastes the quail dish, he remembers eating this delicious dish only once at the Cafe Anglais in Paris. Little does he know that Audran, now living as a cook and servant for the two sisters who took her in 14 years earlier, is the chef who created that dish. The meal is served with some fine rare wines, including an 1845 Clos de Vougeot along with 1860 Veuve Clicquot champagne and other spirits. One of the pleasures of this scene is watching Audran tasting each dish before serving it. Another is how the 12 diners, who arrive with hidden animosities toward each other, are filled with love by the end of the meal.

Annie Hall (1977). The rumor is that this hilarious film only made the cut because a majority of cooking scene nuts are also Woody Allen fans. Even though the lobster Allen and Diane Keaton are trying to cook never makes it into the pot, it is Allen's line when it crawls behind the refrigerator that makes this scene so delicious: "Maybe if I put a little dish of butter sauce here with a nutcracker, it will run out the other side." Oh well, la-di-da, la-di-da, la la.

Julie and Julia (2009). One of the prerequisites for membership on the best cooking scene fan club is being able say *bon appetit* and sound like Meryl Streep imitating Julia Child. Then you have to cook the 524 recipes of *Mastering the Art of French Cooking* in 365 days. If you complain, you are told that if Amy Adams could do it you can. Finally, you have to cook a roast turkey. But first you have to drop the turkey on the kitchen floor, pick it up, put it back in the pan, look at the camera and say, "Remember, you're alone in the kitchen." And that is the scene in this film that fans of cooking scenes relish.

Accidental Tourist (1988). Scratch a cooking scene nut and you will find a romantic. Which is why Bill Pullman, in love with William Hurt's spinster sister (Amy Wright), is the only person at the Thanksgiving dinner willing to eat the undercooked turkey Wright prepares. Happily, Pullman doesn't get food poisoning, lives to play the president of the United States and helps to fight the alien invaders in *Independence Day* (1996).

The Ipcress File (1965). When Harry Palmer (Michael Caine) says to the woman he is about to seduce, "I am going to cook you the best meal you've ever eaten," we know we are in for a great cooking scene. First, he puts on some Mozart, which Harry says is the perfect music to cook by. He puts some butter in the pan, then adds a few eggs and the canned mushrooms. We never know what Harry is cooking, but we suspect that Len Deighton, who wrote the novel on which the film is based, must have been an accomplished cook.

CUTLERY

Spellbound (1945). Gregory Peck, a favorite actor of many film fans, is no favorite of cutlery scene fans. The reason for their displeasure is the scene in which he is dining with Ingrid Bergman at the sanitarium. As she is talking,

Bergman absentmindedly runs a fork over the table linen. Peck keeps staring at the lines the fork makes in the cloth. Visibly upset, he suddenly shouts, "There must be a surplus of table linen in this institution."

Now, by the rules of table etiquette, Bergman should never have used a fork in that way and Peck was probably correct in reprimanding her. But to a cutlery scene fan, it was Bergman who was correct and Peck the poor sport. Not only did Bergman use her cutlery in a striking and original way, but had she not done so, she never would have discovered that, to Peck, the table linen represented snow and the lines the fork made ski trails. More importantly, Peck would never have remembered what he saw in the snow that day.

Beauty and the Beast (1999). It took an animated candlestick who sounds like Maurice Chevalier and a catchy song called "Be Our Guest" to charm cutlery scene fans into adding this scene to the list. The dancing dishes and forks, not to mention those spoons that do a Busby Berkeley synchronized swim number in a soup tureen, not only charmed Belle, but also convinced the entire cutlery scene fan club that a Walt Disney animated cutlery scene deserved its place the category.

How Green Was My Valley (1941). Roddy McDowall not only knew his way around a good bird scene, but he could handle himself in a dramatic knife-and-fork scene as well. The cutlery scene between him and his father (Donald Crisp) in the early part of the film is a masterpiece of timing and nuance. When McDowall's older brothers leave the supper table after a dispute with Crisp, he remains to show his dad he still loves him. How does McDowall express this feeling without words? He bangs his knife and fork on his plate after each mouthful. After three or four bangings, Crisp looks up from his supper and quietly says, "I see you there, my son." Cutlery scene fans, not accustomed to seeing a knife and fork used to express love and devotion, can often be seen weeping with emotion whenever this powerful scene is shown.

DENTIST

Marathon Man (1976). Though it does not take place in a dentist's office, the Dustin Hoffman–Laurence Olivier drilling scene in this John Schlesinger film is enormously popular with dentist scene fans. Unfortunately, the inclusion of this harrowing scene on the list does not make dentist scene fans very popular with dentists. Although resigned to the fact that they are often portrayed as villains, many dentists are particularly unhappy that Olivier uses the novocaine after the drilling, not before, as they are taught to do in dental school. They are also upset by the fact that since the release of this film, no dentist has been able to ask a patient, "Is it safe?"

Little Shop of Horrors (1986). To a dentist scene fan it has everything— a patient so frightened he can hang from the ceiling; another who, when asked to say "ah," cries "argh!" after he sees what is in store for him; and Steve Martin playing a sadistic dentist with all the stops pulled out. Martin finally meets his match when a masochistic patient, played by Bill Murray, walks into his office. Murray can't wait to be drilled. In this inspired scene, he even adjusts the dentist's light and puts in the cotton rolls himself so Martin can get started inflicting pain sooner. Best moment: A tossup between Murray trying to steal a drill on his way out and Martin punching his nurse while singing, "Be a dentist! You have a talent for causing pain." Best line: "Wait, I'm not numb."

10 (1979). Dentist scene fans are still disappointed that Blake Edwards changed the title of his movie about a man's yen for a dentist's daughter from *5* to *10*. Although not generally known, the film was originally called *5* because that is how many fillings Dudley Moore has to submit to in order to get Bo Derek's honeymoon address. The result is tough on Moore but a treat for dentist scene fans, who get to watch a rarity in movies—a five-filling dentist scene.

What finally softened up dentist scene fans enough to vote the scene into the awards category was its residual effects. After leaving the dentist's office, Moore can't drink coffee because he has a mouth full of novocaine; he's unable to talk to Julie Andrews because he has a mouth full of novocaine; and he nearly gets arrested when he can't tell the police he has a mouth full of novo-caine because he has a mouth full of novocaine. One sure way to spot a dentist scene fan, by the way, is if you ever hear someone refer to this film as *5*.

Dark Command (1940). John Wayne has played a lot of roles in westerns but perhaps his most unusual is as an assistant to traveling tooth-puller Doc Grunch (Gabby Hayes). Wayne's job? To provoke people into fights so that he can knock an opponent's tooth loose. Hayes then pulls the loose tooth for a fee and he and Wayne split the proceeds. The movie's all about Quantrill's raiders but that's not what dentist scene fans care about because they always leave the theater before the plot kicks in.

DISAPPEARANCES

Field of Dreams (1989). How about that corn field? The players enter the scene by walking out of it, and when they're through playing baseball, they walk back in and disappear. One of the players wisecracks that he's melting as he walks back in. The guy must have been a *Wizard of Oz* fan. But it's James Earl Jones who's voted the best actor in a disappearance scene. The players invite him in and he wants to know what's in there. Jones tries it first with his arm and then pulls it back out. Then he walks in a step or two, mugs it up a little, and then he walks all the way in. And that's the last we see of him. Kevin Costner isn't invited and he's pissed off. Many in the club think he had a right to be upset. Hey, it was his cornfield.

Star Wars, Episode IV (1977). Maybe James Earl Jones's disappearance in *Field of Dreams* was payback for being the voice of Darth Vadar and making Obi-Wan Kenobi (Alec Guinness) disappear in this film. With a stroke of Vadar's light saber Kenobi disappears and his cloak just falls to the floor. But Guinness warned Vadar that he couldn't win before they started dueling. As Guinness says, "If you strike me down, I shall become more powerful than you can possibly imagine." Yoda ends up the same way, giving disappearance aficionados something else to look forward to in the same film series.

Picnic at Hanging Rock (1975). The problem with disappearance scenes is the question of where exactly does the person who disappears disappear to. The three school girls and their teacher who vanish at a place called Hanging Rock in 1900 Australia can't tell us, because they've disappeared.

The film's director, Peter Weir, can't tell us, because he doesn't know. What he does know is how to make a beautiful and haunting movie.

The Invisible Man (1933). Disappearing on screen can cause some unusual side effects. When Claude Rains tried it, he went insane. This was Rains's first picture, but we don't see a lot of him. James Whale was the director, but it ranks way behind his *Frankenstein, Bride of Frankenstein* and even *Green Hell*.

DUELING

Scaramouche (1952). If the records kept by the dueling fan club secretary had not been lost, the duel between the Marquis de Mayne (Mel Ferrer) and Andre Moreau (Stewart Granger) would certainly be the longest dueling scene in film history. The duelists start in the vestibule of Comedia dell'Arte, make their way to the balcony and then the ledge, and fence all the way to the orchestra and finally to the stage. Though wonderfully choreographed, the duel is so long that two dueling scene fans fell asleep at one screening. They were summarily suspended from the club for two weeks. Because of the splendid swordplay, Stewart Granger and Mel Ferrer are considered to be the equals of Basil Rathbone and Errol Flynn, long regarded as the finest swordsmen in Hollywood.

The Duellists (1977). The longest nonconsecutive duel between the same antagonists takes place during and after the Napoleonic Wars, over a period of fifteen years. The duellists are two French Hussar officers, Keith Carradine and Harvey Keitel. Whatever the quarrel was that started the business in the first place has been long forgotten and the two officers duel with swords and pistols throughout the movie. Keitel is obsessed and pursues every opportunity to find Carradine. This is good news for dueling scene fans, because they finally get to see an entire movie. The final duel is a pursuit through a ruin with each of the protagonists armed with a pair of dueling pistols. When Keitel misses his second shot, Carradine immediately seizes the initiative and corners Keitel at gunpoint, coldly informing him that he has decided to spare his life — on the condition that, since according to the rules of single combat Keitel's life now belongs to him, Keitel must conduct himself in the future as a "dead" person and must never have any further contact whatsoever with Carradine ever again. This was director Ridley Scott's first film. The next movie he directed was *Alien* (1979).

Rob Roy (1995). The betting at the dueling scene fan club is that Tim Roth would have given Stewart Granger a run for his money. But in his duel with Liam Neeson, the poor schmuck pauses to glance at his sponsor, John Hurt. Neeson then grabs the blade of Roth's rapier, picks up his own claymore, and comes up at Roth with a diagonal slash. Blood spilling from his chest and mouth, Roth collapses and dies.

The Adventures of Robin Hood (1938). Errol Flynn and Basil Rathbone have remained on the best dueling scene list for more than 74 years. A large part of this is because of the scene where Flynn has to duel Rathbone in order to rescue the imprisoned Olivia de Haviland. The fight is still thrilling. And the dialogue holds up pretty well. When during the duel Rathbone asks Flynn if he knows any prayers, Flynn replies, "I'll say one for you." The use of shadows during the duel is also a nice touch. The one regret expressed by dueling scene fans is that in all their duels, in all their movies, Rathbone doesn't get to win even once.

Kill Bill: Vol. 1 (2003). Members of the dueling scene fan club who have actually held a sword in their hands point out that a single person fighting 134 masked ninja swordsmen is going to get hurt. Tell that to Uma Thurman, who battles first two, then four, then a horde of ninjas. Before that, she dispatches that cute mace-wielding teenage girl with the plaid skirt and knee socks (although Thurman does plead with the girl to go home and not fight her). The finale is set in a snow-filled garden where Thurman slices the top of Lucy Liu's head off. The dueling scene was so bloody that Quentin Tarantino, the film's director, had to shoot it in black and white.

The Seven-Per-Cent Solution (1976). The 1987 ruling by the club committee that duels were not just for pistols and swords opened the category up to two delightful dueling scenes. The first is the duel between Alan Arkin (who plays Freud) and Jeremy Kemp (the Baron von Leinsdorf). Freud is the injured party and gets to choose the weapons — tennis rackets. The match is played and filmed on one of the historic tennis courts at the Queens Club in West Kensington, London. The match is witnessed by Dr. Watson (Robert Duvall), who points out to Freud that von Leinsdorf's backhand is terrible. Freud not only wins the "duel" but Watson also passes on this information to Sherlock Holmes (Nicol Williamson), which helps him defeat von Leinsdorf in that final duel on the top of a moving train.

Deliverance (1972). The second dueling scene without a sword or pistol in sight includes only a banjo and a guitar. Ronnie Cox, in his first movie role, is fiddling with a few chords on his guitar. A young hillbilly boy sitting on the porch imitates the chords on his banjo. When Cox tries a few simple melodies, the boy with the banjo follows along. Pretty soon the melodies get faster and more difficult. They're so catchy that an old hillbilly starts dancing. The banjo kid smiles for the first time. At the finish, Cox tries to give the hillbilly kid a high five, but the boy turns away providing a nice foreshadowing of the hillbilly rape of Ned Beatty. A pretty rough scene, especially when you consider that this was Beatty's first movie, too.

Crouching Tiger, Hidden Dragon (2000). "This ends right here." Not a very promising beginning to a great dueling scene. But off Jen and Mu Bai go into the tree tops, hopping from tree to tree for their thrilling sword fight. Dueling scene movie nuts, accustomed to suspending disbelief, don't even mind that the branches look as if they could barely support a small bird.

ELEVATOR

True Lies (1994). To be added to the original list of best elevator scenes in film history, an elevator scene has to compete with a drunken ballerina seated in one in *Turning Point* (1978), not to mention Inspector Clouseau's wife Capucine using one as a dressing room to change her wardrobe in *The Pink Panther* (1964). But the elevator scene in *True Lies* not only competes with these great scenes, it also surpasses them. When Arnold Schwarzenegger rode into that hotel elevator on a horse and asked the elderly couple to please press the top button, elevator scene fans went wild and unanimously voted it in.

The Turning Point (1978). This film, which is reported to have done so much for the popularity of ballet in America, didn't do too badly for the popularity of elevators either. The scene that did it for elevators occurs midway through the film. Leslie Browne has just downed six Manhattans because she discovered Mikhail Baryshnikov with another dancer. On her way back to give a performance, there is a quick cut to Anne Bancroft waiting for the backstage elevator. The elevator doors open on Leslie Browne sitting on the floor, quite drunk. She even waves, "Hi."

Elevator scene historians believe this is the first time someone not dead was shown sitting in an elevator. Particularly satisfying to elevator etiquette buffs is the fact that Browne was sitting facing the door. To those who ask what this film actually did for the popularity of elevators, elevator scene statisticians point to this fact: In the year this movie was released, elevator travel was up 120 percent.

The Maltese Falcon (1941). Because elevator scene fans are not usually big on movie symbolism, they don't fully appreciate the final dramatic elevator scene in this classic film noir. Humphrey Bogart has just told Mary Astor that he won't play the sap for her. That because she hasn't played straight with him for one second, he's sending her over. Bogart then puts Astor into the elevator and watches it descend. The camera lingers on her looking at Bogart through the elevator's bars. The more intuitive among elevator scene fans recognize that the small elevator symbolizes the jail cell where Astor will spend the next twenty years. There are more than a few fans of this timeless film who have threatened to send their kids over when they discover that all the times they said they brushed their teeth, all they did was wet their toothbrushes and move the toothpaste to the other side of the sink.

The Pink Panther (1963). Even rarer than horses in elevators is elevator dressing. (This is elevator scene fan parlance for turning an elevator into a dressing room.) It is pulled off quite smartly by Inspector Clouseau's wife, the beautiful actress Capucine. After being spotted by the Paris police, she quickly ducks into an office building elevator; turns her suit jacket inside out; changes her hat; shoes and handbag' and emerges from the same elevator in a completely different outfit. Elevator scene fans have attempted to duplicate Capucine's performance in a variety of elevators throughout the nation, but to date have been unable to report any great success.

Lady in a Cage (1964). Elevators have feelings, too. That is the premise of this disturbing thriller starring Olivia de Havilland and James Caan (his screen debut). When the elevator in de Havilland's mansion breaks down with her inside, she reprimands it very sharply by exclaiming, "Oh, what's the matter with you?" This results in an elevator huff, which results in de Havilland being trapped in a sulky elevator. She doesn't like this at all because all sorts of people break into the house and terrorize her. Elevator scene fans like it though, because the elevator is on screen for practically the entire movie.

Best moment: When de Havilland throws her shoe through the elevator bars at the ringing telephone (a movie first).

Dressed to Kill (1980). Angie Dickinson has done for elevators what Janet Leigh did for showers—she made people afraid to go into one. It is no secret that there was a lot of support for consigning this scene to film oblivion—the reason being that elevator scene fans do not ordinarily favor elevator scenes that show elevators in a bad light. Still, elevator murder is most rare, and when tastefully done it can be quite thrilling. This is why they agreed to consider it. The vote was close, the deciding factor being director Brian De Palma's stylish handling of the stabbing, which was accomplished without messing up the interior of the elevator. It is interesting to note that in *Psycho* (1960), Hitchcock doesn't let his victim mess up the shower either. Elevator scene moralists like to point to two other similarities between these two films—both murderers are dressed as women and both actresses play characters who are carrying on an illicit affair.

The Untouchables (1987). Only an elevator scene movie nut would figure out that Brian De Palma, who also directed *Dressed to Kill*, had a thing for elevator murder. In this film, he has a mob gunman shoot Charles Martin Smith in a police station elevator and then has him write "touchable" in Smith's blood in the elevator wall.

An actress held in especially high regard by elevator scene fans for her uncanny ability to publicize elevators is Audrey Hepburn. While playing the role of Princess Ann in *Roman Holiday* (1953), she walks into Gregory Peck's room after escaping from her castle, takes one look at it, and casually remarks, "Is this the elevator?"

FALSE TEETH

Crossing Delancey (1987). Though Hollywood's lack of courage in this genre has limited false teeth scenes mostly to shots of them in half-filled glasses of water, it hasn't stopped actors with the right false teeth sensibility from occasionally turning one into a scene that thrills the audience. That is precisely what happens when Amy Irving's bubba gives Peter Reichart his whiskey in a glass containing a set of lowers. Reichart, who could have ruined the scene by going "Yecch," instead made it immortal with the reaction of an actor who truly knows his way around a false teeth scene. When she hands him the glass, he calmly remarks, "I said whiskey neat, not on the rocks."

Starting Over (1979). While false teeth fans prefer to see an actual denture, they are not averse to scenes in which false teeth are merely mentioned, as long as they are mentioned in a favorable light. A good example of this occurs in the final scene of this appealing comedy when Burt Reynolds asks Jill Clayburgh to marry him. In his proposal, he lists all the things he would like to do together with Clayburgh, including a wish to see their dentures in the same glass when they are old. "That's what I want. What do you want?" Reynolds asks. Clayburgh then responds with a line that endeared her to health-conscious false teeth fans everywhere. "I want my own glass."

For the record, marriage proposal fans: did put in a claim for this scene, but it was quickly dropped when false teeth fans, possessive about their territory, threatened to have every actor and actress in every winning marriage proposal scene checked for dentures.

Help! (1965). When the crazed-looking man in the Beatles's apartment releases two sets of fake false teeth that go chattering across the rug toward the camera, some film fans feel it is just a cheap attempt to get a laugh. False teeth fans find this attitude ridiculous and insulting—another example of how people put down the genre. To them, it seems obvious that both the man and the false teeth have a role to play. The man is a dowser and the false teeth are looking for a glass of water.

Midnight Cowboy (1969). Although at least one false teeth scene escaped from the ubiquitous glass of water, it took an ugly encounter between the normally sweet Jon Voight and Bernard Hughes to pull it off. While the shot of Hughes's false teeth coming loose after Voight hit him for nonpayment of services rendered is considered a classic, false teeth fans would have settled for Hughes biting into an apple to get the shot. This admission took a certain amount of courage. It was a confession that false teeth fans, lulled by too many shots of uppers and lowers in too many glasses of water, were not yet ready for a false teeth scene in the midst of a homosexual encounter.

FEATHER

Four Feathers (1939). I never knew that white feathers symbolize cowardice until I saw this film. So whenever I see one on the sidewalk, I try to do something brave, then look for the pigeon it came from and give it back. That's what Harry Faversham does in this film. When three of his fellow officers give him white feathers after he resigns his commission on the eve of a big battle, he poses as a mute and rescues them after they are captured. Only then is he able to give them the feathers back. The fourth feather is symbolic — Faversham's fiancée breaks their engagement. That "feather" Faversham gives back by marrying her. Members of the feather scene fan club who have been through a messy divorce say the return of that "feather" may have been a big mistake.

Forrest Gump (1994). Feathers do a lot better here. Feather scene enthusiasts like to point out that in this movie they symbolize destiny and blind dumb luck. That opening sequence where the camera tracks a feather floating in the air until it finally lands on Tom Hanks's shoe is quite beautiful. So is the music that goes along with it. It's no surprise when Hanks picks that feather up, and puts it in his suitcase to keep.

FISHING

A report in the *New York Times* that style-conscious women looking for long colorful feathers to arrange in their hair had created a shortage and forced up the price for fly fishermen who use the same feathers for fly tying was read at the latest fishing scene fan club meeting. The news cast such a pall on the membership that they decided to lighten up the mood with their first choice.

Funny Farm (1988). No, the favorite scene is not the snake that Chevy Chase catches when he goes fishing in the lake for trout. It's the fishing scene in the rowboat when Chase hooks the neck of one of his fellow anglers. To get the hook out, Chase decides to knock him out so it won't hurt. That doesn't work and the poor guy winds up jumping overboard and swimming to shore.

A River Runs Through It (1992). Brad Pitt may not be such a hot poker player, owing money to nearly everyone in western Montana, but he is the best fly fisherman that fishing scene fans have ever seen. To a fishing scene nut, the section of the film that shows Pitt casting in a way never seen before, then hooking a trout that's big enough to pull him down the river and through the rapids, is worth the price of admission alone. It's all most fishing scene fans ever see or want to see of this beautiful film, so they are spared having to hear that Pitt gets beaten up and killed by the poker thugs he owes money to.

Jaws (1975). "You're going to need a bigger boat." When Roy Scheider says that to Robert Shaw after he sees the shark for the first time, this becomes more of a horror flick than a fishing flick. Fishing scene fans tend to agree because no one goes fishing with a revolver or blows a shark to pieces by shooting a bullet into the scuba tank he wedges into its mouth.

The Quiet Man (1952). To a fishing scene fan, it is not John Wayne's fight with Maureen O'Hara that makes them want to watch this movie. Nor is it Wayne's fight with Squire Will Danaher (Victor McLaglen) that lures them in. It is Ward Bond's fight with the fish he's been trying to catch for a long time. He finally hooks it, and then he loses it and lets out a curse in Gaelic. The conversation Bond has with Maureen O'Hara afterward is interesting, too. But not to members of the fishing scene fan club. And not because it's in Gaelic. Fishing scene fans always leave the theater right after Bond loses the fish. For those fishing scene nuts who are curious about movie scenes outside of fishing, what O'Hara was telling Bond (the parish priest) was that she makes John Wayne sleep in a sleeping bag. She said it in Gaelic because she was too embarrassed to say it in English.

Deliverance (1972). The voting was contentious and took all night. Finally, shortly before 4 A.M., the scene of Burt Reynolds fishing from his canoe was finally voted in as one of the best fishing scenes in movie history. The sticking point for many members of the club was that Reynolds was fishing for trout with a bow and arrow. He was successful on the second try and the four men had the trout for dinner.

Salmon Fishing in the Yemen (2011). Love is like swimming upstream, point out the romantics among fishing scene movie fans. Sure, Emily Blunt is easy to fall in love with, but what won over members of the club was Ewan McGregor's skill at hooking an assassin in the neck just as he was about to shoot Sheik Mohammad. However, those in the club who have actually fished for salmon were more taken with the scenes in which McGregor goes salmon fishing by day and at night dines in a black-tie ensemble on the salmon he caught.

With apologies to Mr. Hemingway, the fishing scene fan club regrets it has not included *The Old Man and the Sea* (1958) for the simple reason that the scenes where Spencer Tracy was supposed to be fishing in the open sea were shot in a studio tank. *Moby Dick* (1956) was left off the list for a different reason. Simply put, whaling is not fishing.

FLOWER

The Big Sleep (1946). From the moment Philip Marlowe (Humphrey Bogart) enters General Sternwood's (Charles Waldron) hothouse, we know we're in for a great flower scene. Neither man likes the orchids. As Sternwood says, "Their flesh is too much like the flesh of humans." Because of the orchids, the hothouse is humidified like a sauna. Marlowe begins sweating the moment he enters. The General encourages Marlowe to remove his outer coat, loosen his tie, and drink and smoke to his heart's delight. The General also confesses to a vicarious pleasure he receives simply from watching Marlowe indulge in the vices that he can no longer enjoy due to his health. It should be noted that before the flower scene fan club members watch this scene, they turn the thermostat up so they can sweat right along with Marlowe.

Little Shop of Horrors (1986). Feed me! The flower in this movie is one green mother from outer space and she's bad! Why else would Rick Moranis tell her he's given her sunlight, he's given her rain but all she wants him to do is to open a vein? Flower scene fans get a kick out of the fact that the plant is named Audrey.

Alice in Wonderland (2010). There's only one thing to do when a deck of playing cards plants white roses by mistake and the Red Queen (Helena Bonham Carter) likes them red. They paint the roses red, knowing that if the Queen sees white roses, it's off with their heads. Flower scene fans usually walk out before the scene ends because they know that when you paint white roses red, they will not only cease to grow, but pretty soon they'll be dead.

The Seven-Per-Cent Solution (1976). It is a trail of lilies that Lila Deveraux (Vanessa Redgrave) leaves for Sherlock Holmes (Nicol Williamson) to follow that helps him solve the mystery of her kidnapping. It is rare that a flower scene plays such an important role in a movie. The lilies that Redgrave throws out the hansom cab's window lead Holmes and Watson (played by Robert Duvall) to the train station, where they hijack a private train to follow Redgrave. The duel that Holmes fights with Baron Karl von Leinsdorf (Jeremy Kemp) in this charming comedy adventure is thrilling. Had Kemp known that the lilies he gave Redgrave would lead to his downfall, he would never have bought them for her.

City Lights (1931). It's a good thing this is a silent movie because the sobbing when club members watch that final scene would have drowned out any dialogue. No dialogue is needed to express the emotions of the two stars. When Chaplin passes the store window and recognizes the once blind flower girl, he just stares at her with a flower in his hand. The petals drop, one by one. She looks up, offers him a flower, and tries to give him a coin. When she feels his hand, then his face, she realizes it is the Little Tramp who paid for the operation that cured her blindness. There is only one word of dialogue on the screen: "You!" The Little Tramp nods and the film ends with them looking at each other with love. After the film, many in the club go to Tulip's, the bar down the street, to discuss how lucky Chaplin was not to be Humphrey Bogart. In *High Sierra* (1941), after Bogart pays for the operation to fix Joan Leslie's club foot, she dumps him for an insurance salesman.

Visitors to the flower fans' clubhouse are always surprised to see a life-size photo of Sabu above the fireplace. The photo is there to remind them that in the movie masterpiece *Black Narcissus* (1947), the title does not refer to a flower but rather the name of the cheap scent Sabu bought in an Army Navy store in London. As the Young General tells Deborah Kerr, "It's so common to smell of ourselves, don't you think?"

FLUTTERING DRAPES

Lost Horizon (1937). In Hollywood, fluttering drapes have been used to symbolize many things, the most interesting being the death of Sam Jaffe. In this distinguished film set in Shangri-La, fluttering drape fans are quick to point out that when Jaffe (as the high lama) finally gives up the ghost, it is the fluttering drapes, not the candle going out, that tips off Ronald Colman and the audience that Jaffe is dead. Admirers of this memorable scene credit the movie's director, Frank Capra, with such great camera work that one can almost see Jaffe's soul floating out the window.

The Uninvited (1947). By the time this film was made, fluttering drape scenes had so evolved that they were able to bring to a stop both haunting crying sounds and the smell of mimosa. Every night, when Gail Russell went to sleep, she heard the crying and smelled the mimosa. The crying and the smell of mimosa went on all night until the dawn breeze made the drapes on her windows flutter. When the drapes began to flutter, the crying and the smell of mimosa stopped. Russell was very grateful. It meant she could finally get to sleep.

The World of Henry Orient (1964). A set designer's goof nearly cost this charming movie its rightful place in fluttering drape history. The scene almost lost to us is the Peter Sellers–Paula Prentiss "fluttering drape seduction scene." It appears in quotes because the drapes never fluttered. The drapes never fluttered because a distracted set designer (his car having been towed away that morning) misread the word "diaphanous" as "denim." As a result, Sellers had to peak through the drapes to spot Tippy Walker and Merrie Spaeth sitting on the steps across the street. The original shooting script has Sellers spotting them through fluttering, diaphanous drapes. Only the chance discovery of the now retired set designer's diary saved this scene from oblivion.

Black Narcissus (1947). When Deborah Kerr tells David Farrar, "It's the wind," her words are enough to set the heart of even the most casual fluttering drape scene fan aflutter. Kerr is trying to explain the cause of the sexual tension she and the sisters are experiencing in that convent so high in the Himalayas. But fluttering drape scene fans aren't interested in that sort of stuff. They are interested in wind, one of the two main elements of a good fluttering drape scene.

Since the wind in this part of the Himalayas blows seven days a week, all that remains to get a good fluttering drape scene is drapes. Happily, there are more drapes in this mountaintop convent than a fluttering drape fan can shake a curtain rod at. We learn as much during the opening scene when Ayah, the old caretaker, is seen running through the remote mountain mission while the camera catches every fluttering drape on every window. From that point on there is hardly a scene in which a drape does not flutter. They are used quite nicely to heighten the already charged atmosphere and play a key role in the scene in which one of the sisters goes mad.

Rebecca (1940). Had it not been for the fluttering drapes in this Academy Award winner, Joan Fontaine might have listened to Mrs. Danvers and jumped from her bedroom window. Judith Anderson, who played Mrs. Danvers, had some pretty strong arguments. Laurence Olivier would never have loved her as he did the first Mrs. DeWinter. And it would have been so easy to jump. Fontaine was about to do so, but the fluttering of the window drapes distracted and brought her to her senses. That is the opinion of a surprising number of fluttering drape fans, many of whom have watched this scene over a dozen times. A small group of fans are of the opinion that Alfred Hitchcock, the film's director, may have wanted Fontaine to jump and reshot the scene without drapes. Reports of fans seeing this drapeless version still circulate in fluttering drape circles.

FOOD MUSHING

Close Encounters of the Third Kind (1977). Yes, the mashed potato sculpture that Richard Dreyfuss makes before he leaves his wife (Terri Garr) is definitely food being mushed. Yes, the potatoes are shaped into a pretty good replica of the isolated area in the wilderness where the aliens will land.

And yes, only Dreyfuss's fork and fingers are used to create the mashed potato mountain. However, this iconic scene is not only of interest to food mushing fans. Since the film's release, divorce lawyers have reported that an increasing number of their clients claim that the partner who has left them built a sculpture out of mashed potatoes before they took off.

The Treasure of the Sierra Madre (1948). Nobody knew how to push beans around a plate like Walter Huston, who in his heyday was the only bankable food mushing superstar in Hollywood. Food mushing fans say that Huston was so good that if you listen carefully, you can hear a definite contrapuntal rhythm between his fork scraping the metal plate and his repeated food mushing entreaties to Tim Holt and Humphrey Bogart as they sit around the campfire. "Want some beans?" Scrape, scrape. "Better have some beans, boys." Scrape, scrape, scrape. "You sure you won't have some beans?" Scrape, scrape. It is a memorable food mushing moment and one that makes it clear that if Holt and Bogart had been eating their beans, they wouldn't have been too exhausted to sit around the campfire and mush food with Huston.

Sitting Pretty (1948). The food mushing scene in this film is so seductive that even the urbane Clifton Webb finds it impossible not to join the fun. Though Webb never cracks a smile, food mushing fans insist he enjoys it even when the baby throws cereal at him. Webb's lips do form what appears to be a smirk when he retaliates and dumps a bowl of cereal on the baby's head. Food mushing fans explain Webb's rare show of emotion this way: Watching food being mushed is never as much fun as mushing it yourself.

Papillon (1973). Some food mushing scenes are not for the fainthearted. This is especially true when they are set in a solitary confinement cell on Devil's Island. Food mushing fans, however, are not easily revolted. So when Steve McQueen is put on half rations for not squealing on Dustin Hoffman, he shows he can mush food in a revolting way with the best of them. The fact that the "food" he mushes is beetles and grasshoppers in no way violates Rule 3 in the newly revised *Food Mushing Manual*. In essence, Rule 3 states that to be eligible for a food mushing award, an actor may mush anything as long as it is eventually eaten.

Brighton Beach Memoirs (1986). Where else would you expect to find the most original food mushing moment in film history but Brooklyn? More specifically, the Brooklyn of Neil Simon's boyhood, circa 1937. But even in Brooklyn, great food mushing scenes aren't that easy to put together. First, liver has to be on the menu for dinner. Second, the liver has to be tough and it has to be served with mashed potatoes. Then, the actor it's served to (Jonathan Silverman) has to not like liver and bury it in his mashed potatoes when he thinks his mother isn't looking. Finally, he has to have a sharp-eyed mother (Blythe Danner), who tells him to eat the liver under his mashed potatoes. Funniest exchange? When Danner says to her son, "Why did you take the liver if you didn't like it?" and her son replies, "I didn't take it. It came with the plate."

Of Mice and Men (1939). Food mushing scenes can also be dangerous. Bob Steele finds that out in this classic study of what watching milk being mixed with apple pie can do to someone who is dull-witted. The award-winning scene is wonderfully orchestrated by director Lewis Milestone. First, Steele pours the milk over his apple pie with a great show. Then, he starts to mush it up with his spoon. From Steele's expression, it's easy to see he knows this will infuriate Lennie (played by Lon Chaney, Jr.) but he hasn't the remotest idea of how much. This is only the midpoint of the action and already food mushing fans are anticipating the next dish. They do not have long to wait. A few seconds later, Lennie crushes the hand Steele used to mush his milk and apple pie to a pulp. Considered an especially nice touch is Milestone's use of the apple pie and milk combination to foreshadow the coming violence.

Down and Out in Beverly Hills (1986). The most unselfish food musher in film history is Nick Nolte. To get the family dog (Matisse) to eat his dog food, Nolte gets down on his hands and knees, puts his face into the dog food bowl and starts eating. Matisse, seeing how much Nolte is enjoying the meal, trots over and joins Nolte at the food bowl. Food mushing fans agree this is a very satisfying food mushing scene to watch, but not to try.

No collection of great food mushing scenes would be complete without a special nod to Jeannie Berlin, who in the movie *The Heartbreak Kid* (1972) ordered an egg salad sandwich on her honeymoon and ate it so sloppily that Charles Grodin, her husband of two days, left her to pursue Cybill Shepherd.

Though sloppily eaten sandwiches are not technically food mushing scenes, it was felt that Berlin's sacrifice to the art of food mushing should be noted.

This cleared the way for a special food mushing award to be given Gene Hackman, who in *The French Connection* (1970) had the grace not to be overly annoyed at having to gobble down a street vendor's hot dog while watching drug smuggler Fernando Rey through a restaurant window dining on what looks to be a pretty decent French meal.

Meetings of the food mushing fan club always end with a ritual toast to James Cagney. Cagney, of course, is the actor who "smushed" a half-grapefruit into Mae Clark's face when she began to nudge him in *Public Enemy* (1931). The scene is now considered to be the standard by which all other food mushing scenes are judged.

FUNNY WALK

To Have and Have Not (1944). Fans of funny walks like to say that Walter Brennan practiced his funny walk so much that he knew it backward and forward. That is literally true. In one marvelous scene Brennan does his funny walk both forward and backward and makes it seem fresh each time. He does it forward on his way into the bar to ask Humphrey Bogart for drink money and backward away from the bar when he sees Bogart being escorted out by the Vichy police. Funny walk fans especially appreciate the fact that Brennan was able to reverse his funny walk without missing a beat. They cannot agree, however, whether the walk consisted of two steps and a hop or three steps and a hop. What they do agree on is that it is a very funny walk and the scene is one that is likely to be remembered for a very long time.

Belles of St. Trinian's (1946). Had I not seen a sign on the clubhouse door that read, "FUNNY WALK SCENE DEADLINE IS 5 P.M.," the funny walk in this British import might have been lost to movie fans forever. As a lapsed member of the funny walk scene fan club, I still had voting privileges and, though I had not seen this film in quite a while, proposed it for an award. I described to my fellow funny walk scene fans a character in this film named "Flash Harry" whom I seem to remember was played by George Cole. Harry would wait in the woods outside St. Trinian's for a signal from its headmistress, delightfully played by Alastair Sims. When Sims gave the signal, Harry would put his hands into the pockets of his long overcoat and glide across the lawn to the school. His steps were always in sync with a catchy background tune that was only played when Harry did his walk. When asked to imitate the walk, I could not. Instead, I compared it to a dance performed by the Moiseyev Dance Company in which men in floor-length coats glide across the stage. What made the dance so remarkable was that you never saw their legs moving. So it was with Harry's walk. You never saw his legs moving.

The Hunchback of Notre Dame (1939). Quasimodo's goofy walk as he follows Esmeralda through the streets of fifteenth-century Paris greatly endeared Charles Laughton to funny walk scene fans here in the United States. Funny walk scene insiders report there are two theories to explain the origin of Laughton's funny walk. The first, and most widely held, is that it was caused by Laughton's fake hump, which may have thrown off his gait. The second theory, just recently formulated, is that Laughton sprained his ankle while lying on his back ecstatically kicking the bells after Maureen O'Hara gave him a drink of water on the pillory. This theory was formed when it was noticed that Laughton began favoring his left leg, transforming his walk into a definite lope. Since Laughton kept no funny walk diary, it is unlikely that either theory will ever be proven.

Young Frankenstein (1974). That funny walk scene fans should choose a scene based on one of the oldest jokes in history shows they have no shame. Still, when it is done right, the old "walk this way" routine can result in a very funny walk indeed. When Marty Feldman, who plays Igor carrying a very short cane, tells Gene Wilder to "walk this way," and then bends over each time he uses the cane, funny walk scene fans howl. When Wilder just follows him, prompting Feldman to say, "No, walk *this* way," and demonstrates, they howl even louder. And when Wilder finally walks the way Feldman walks, they are convulsed. Funny walk scene historians report that the question "What would people think of this selection?" never came up during the voting. Apparently, there is just one thing that counts in a funny walk scene: *Is the walk funny?* It is.

House Calls (1978). Fans of funny walk scenes have been expecting Walter Matthau to win a funny walk award for more than two decades. No actor ever had such a naturally funny walk or showed so much promise. Unhappily, Matthau never lived up to that promise until he got the opportunity to go jogging with Glenda Jackson. His walk in that scene was so comic and original it earned him this long-awaited laurel and rewarded the patience of funny walk scene fans across the nation. What may have finally put him over the top, report funny walk scene theorists, was Matthau's attempt to run in order to keep up with Jackson. I am inclined to agree.

Monty Python and the Holy Grail (1974). The sound of horses' hooves in the mist is not a very promising situation in which to find a funny walk. Nor is the sight of knights' heads bobbing as they come into sight. But if, when they finally appear in full view, it turns out to be John Cleese leading a group of knights who have no horses, the situation is indeed promising. Cleese and the knights are not knights on horseback at all — they are imitating knights on horseback by walking funny.

At this point it might be worth noting that the selection of this scene caused quite a heated discussion. Many funny walk scene fans have not yet forgiven Cleese for his "Ministry of Silly Walks" skit on public television. Since "Silly Walks" first aired, funny walk scene club members have become the butt of many jokes. That club members were able to rise above their personal feelings and select this scene shows that funny walk scene fans take funny walks seriously. What may finally have clinched it for Cleese were the men following behind the knights banging coconuts together so the funny walks would sound like horses galloping.

Mr. Hulot's Holiday (1953). A favorite of funny walk scene fans since he began walking funny in *Jour de Fête* (1949), Jacques Tati's funny walk reached its peak in this joyous French comedy. Tati's self-conscious walk (on tip toes, with his upper body forward) is best described by imagining what a rather shy ostrich would look like if he were unsure of where he was going or whether he would be welcome when he arrived. Tati is so revered by funny walk fans that they saved his scene for last.

GREED

Funny Farm (1988). There is a scene near the beginning of this film that puts it on the very top of the Best Greed Scenes in Film History list (and that includes *Greed* and *Wall Street*). Chevy Chase has given up his job as a sportswriter and he and his wife have bought a house in Vermont. But they arrive before the moving van. No furniture and no food. Chase tells his wife he thinks there's an apple left for them to eat. She tells him no, they already ate it. They go to bed on the floor. In the middle of the night Chase wakes up because he hears the crunch of an apple on his wife's side of the floor. The scene has been placed at the top of the list because members of the club feel it transcends selfishness and heads into an area beyond greed — into the mysterious and complicated relationship between husbands and wives.

Wall Street (1987). "Greed, for lack of a better word, is good. Greed is right. Greed works. Greed clarifies, cuts through, and captures the essence of the evolutionary spirit." So says Gordon Gekko. It got him a beautiful wife and a house in the Hamptons, and an Oscar for Michael Douglas, the actor who played him. The scene that greed movie nuts love most is when Charlie Sheen and Douglas are riding in Gekko's limousine and Gekko points to a building and tells Sheen that the $800,000 he made selling it was better than the best orgasm he ever had. Of course, greed got Gordon Gekko one more thing: it got him sent to jail.

Key Largo (1948). Edward G. Robinson, who plays the gangster Johnny Rocco in this movie, not only knows his way around a good cigar, he also knows he is greedy. When Lauren Bacall asks him what he wants in storming in and taking over their hotel, Bogart tells her he knows what Rocco wants: "Rocco wants more. Isn't that right, Rocco?" Robinson takes the cigar out of his mouth and has what club members call a greed epiphany: "More, yeah. That's what I want. More!"

Wall Street: Money Never Sleeps (2010). Edward G. Robinson isn't the only actor who wants more. There's a nice little scene in this film where Shia LaBeouf asks Wall Street biggie Josh Brolin what his number is. Brolin thinks LaBeouf is asking what his starting salary will be. LaBeouf explains that what he is actually asking Brolin is how much money it would take for him to walk away and retire: "Everyone's got a number and they always know the exact amount. So what's yours?" Brolin smiles and tells him what his number is: "more." Greed movie nuts always like it when scenes like this show that young screenwriters are still watching the old classics.

It's a Mad, Mad, Mad World (1963). Greed hurts. The search for $350,000 buried under the W lands Sid Caesar, Milton Berle, Terry Thomas,

Phil Silvers, Buddy Hackett, Mickey Rooney, Jonathon Winters and Dick Shawn in the hospital. Jimmy Durante, whose dying words started the crazy chase in the first place, didn't do too well either. He kicked the bucket — literally. And Durante isn't the only actor who died because they were greedy. Walter Slezak found that out in *Sinbad the Sailor* (1947) when he refused to share the treasure buried in a pool on the island of Deryabar. But perhaps the most famous greed death was that of Fred C. Dobbs (Humphrey Bogart), who was killed by Alfonso Bedoya's machete in *The Treasure of the Sierra Madre*. Bedoya, who only wanted Dobbs's mules, likewise suffered: he was shot by a Mexican firing squad.

Though the greed fan club is said to be in possession of the lost 10-hour version of Erich von Stroheim's 1924 silent film masterpiece, *Greed*, they still can't make heads or tails out of the plot. So, as proud as they are of having a film named after their fan club, it could not be voted in.

HAIRCUT

The Treasure of the Sierra Madre (1948). Who would have thought that Humphrey Bogart would have such exquisite barbershop manners? The haircut he receives in that Mexican barbershop may just be one of the three worst haircuts in film history. Yet when the barber shows Bogart how it looks in the back, he meekly nods, "Okay." Why?

Some haircut scene fans feel that Bogart simply didn't want to hurt the barber's feelings. Others argue that the director, John Huston, held Bogart in a tight rein in order to make his anger against Tim Holt more convincing. But a growing minority of haircut scene fans explain Bogart's blind acceptance of "the haircut," as it is now referred to in haircut scene circles, by theorizing that Bogart didn't care how he looked because he knew he wasn't going to make it out of the film alive.

Hannah and Her Sisters (1986). Maureen O'Sullivan is beloved by haircut scene fans for delivering what they consider to be the best haircut line in film history. Turning to her husband, Lloyd Nolan, she refers to him as "this haircut that passes for a man." In one devastating line, O'Sullivan is able to evoke all the expensive haircuts Nolan got during their troubled marriage in order to look better to all the women he had affairs with. Since there is no mention in the Haircut Scene Rule Book about a haircut scene actually having to be in a movie to be eligible, the scene was voted onto the list on the strength of a single line of dialogue.

Roman Holiday (1953). Tullio Carminati, Audrey Hepburn's Italian barber, was so impressed with the haircut he gave her that he asked Hepburn to go dancing. This barber-customer date is a screen first, not repeated again until *Shampoo* in 1975. Haircut scene fans were especially impressed with Carminati's ability to sweat while cutting Hepburn's hair (to show he didn't approve of how much she wanted to take off). Carminati's use of the word "off" each time he took a snip and his repeated questioning of Hepburn, "Are you sure, Miss?," nearly won him a Golden Scissors award. Haircut scene purists who require a good haircut before voting a scene its award needn't have worried. Not even the Demon Barber of Fleet Street could make Audrey Hepburn look anything less than lovely.

Wizard of Oz (1939). Haircut scene fans are continuously amazed at how a film that features witches, wizards and flying monkeys makes room for a nifty little haircut scene. It occurs when Dorothy (Judy Garland), the Cowardly Lion (Bert Lahr), the Tin Man (Jack Haley), Scarecrow (Ray Bolger) and Toto reach the Emerald City. Bolger gets more straw, Lahr gets his mane permed and ribbons added, Haley gets simonized, and Garland gets her hair cut and curled. Even Toto gets spruced up.

Each "haircut" is performed to the accompaniment of a delightful song. In one song the lyrics include the classic haircut line, "With a snip, snip here, and a snip, snip there." Another song blends the familiar haircut words, "Snip, snip, snip," with "Buzz, buzz, buzz." Though the lady barbers sing a good tune, not a lock of hair seems to be cut. Still, when confronted with a haircut scene of such charm, and one that includes what is generally regarded as the first dog haircut in screen history, not even the staunchest of haircut scene purists objected to its award.

Jailhouse Rock (1957). One of the best examples of haircut foreshadowing occurs in this early Elvis Presley movie when a woman at a bar says to Presley, "You got nice hair." Before we know it, Presley is in a jail cell waiting to get a haircut. The tension heightens markedly when his cellmate, Mickey Shaughnessy, tells Presley that prison barbers being what they are, it will cost him three packs of cigarettes to get a good haircut. It is at this point in the film that haircut scene fans in the audience usually throw cigarette packs at the screen. Some of these must have gotten to the barber who gives good haircuts, because when Presley gets his haircut (a scene that lasts all of three seconds), he just gets a little taken off the sides. Not to worry. Whatever was taken off grows back remarkably quickly (within the next ten minutes). All of which tends to leave haircut scene fans unsatisfied, but puts Presley fans into a state of near bliss, since his singing seems to improve at the same rate his hair grows back.

In a special ceremony that took place after the voting, a pair of Golden Scissors awards were given out for uncommon valor during a haircut. The first went to Gregory Peck for his superb work in *The Omen* (1976). While giving his son a haircut, Peck continued to cut after discovering the "666" that he suspected was on the boy's scalp was actually there, marking his son as the Antichrist. A second Golden Scissors went to a very young Dean Stockwell, who in *The Boy with Green Hair* (1948) agreed to have his head shaved when nobody liked the color green that his hair turned. A few silent tears were noted by the awards panel, but given Stockwell's age at the time, it did not affect their admiration.

Before finally adjourning, haircut scene fans awarded Dirk Bogarde a rare Platinum Scissors. Bogarde (*Death in Venice*, 1971) won this honor for his courage in remaining in Venice to keep a barbershop appointment even though he knew there was an outbreak of typhus in the city. The award was given posthumously, since Bogarde lost his life on the Lido beach in a beautifully acted final moment, with much of the barber's recently applied mascara running down his face.

HANDCUFF

The 39 Steps (1935). Regarded by handcuff scene historians as the antecedent of all movie handcuff scenes is the moment when the spies (posing as policeman) handcuff Robert Donat to Madeleine Carroll. Admirers of this category point first to the scene in which Donat and Carroll check into the small inn, when. Carroll has to sign the register because she is the one whose right hand is free. But what admirers of handcuff scenes are really waiting for is the moment Carroll has to take off her wet stockings and Donat's handcuffed hand is forced to brush against her leg.

The Defiant Ones (1958). What is it about handcuff scenes? When escaped chain-gang prisoners Tony Curtis and Sidney Poitier are chained together, they hate each other. By the time they have gotten rid of their chains, they are best friends. Maybe we should ask Madeleine Carroll, who dislikes Robert Donat while they are handcuffed but falls in love with him when she is no longer attached to him. The final scene when Poitier's hand reaches out to Curtis from a moving freight train is thrilling. Hard to believe that Stanley Kramer made this Academy Award film in 1958.

Take the Money and Run (1969). Though leg irons are not technically handcuffs, members of the handcuff scene fan club allowed this scene's inclusion because Woody Allen had good reason to escape from the chain gang: they wouldn't let him faint without written permission. The scene after Allen and four fellow convicts escape is the club's favorite. Allen's chain-gang shuffle, seen when he and his pals enter the old lady's home, was vetted by Paul Muni, a former fugitive from a chain gang, and found to be flawless.

The French Connection (1971). Handcuff scene fans are pretty picky about their choices and only gave an honorable mention to the handcuff scene in this tense, action-packed movie. The general feeling in the club was that Gene Hackman doesn't seem too concerned when he wakes up with his foot handcuffed to the bedpost or by the beautiful girl who runs into the bathroom.

HANGING

Kind Hearts and Coronets (1949). Though it is Alec Guinness who gets to be killed eight times in this black comedy masterpiece, it is Dennis Price who gets to be hanged. We know this right from the start when the hangman tells the warden he has never had the privilege of hanging a duke, then asks what the correct form of address is. He is informed it is "Your Grace." Though the hanging fan club never gets to see Price, now the tenth Duke of D'Ascoyne, hanged, they know it is coming because when he is released from prison for the one murder he did not commit, he realizes he has left a memoir in his cell describing all the murders that he did.

True Grit (2010). The Coen brothers more than make up for the hanging gap in *Kind Hearts and Coronets* by giving us three hangings right at the start. Putting the hood over one of the Indians who is getting hanged just as he is about to give his speech was a brilliant touch.

The Ox-Bow Incident (1943). Seems as if Hollywood likes to hang them three at a time. The hanging scene in this western is technically a lynching scene. These tend to embarrass fans of hanging scenes, especially when the men (in this case, Dana Andrews, Anthony Quinn and Francis Ford) are innocent. When Henry Fonda, playing a drifter who joined the posse, tries to stop it, he is told that technically this is none of his business. Every member of the hanging scene fan club knows what Fonda says next: "Hanging's any man's business that's around." Though Fonda couldn't stop the execution of an innocent man this time, members of the hanging scene fan club like to point out that this film is where he got the impetus to do it in *12 Angry Men* (1957).

Tom Jones (1963). Hanging scene movie nuts are also good sports and did not mind Hugh Griffith galloping up to the gallows to rescue Albert Finney moments before he was to be hanged. Ditto for Eugene Pallette rescuing Errol Flynn from the gallows in *The Adventures of Robin Hood* (1938).

The Russians Are Coming, the Russians Are Coming (1966). Any scene where an old man is eating, only to finally turn around, see his wife tied up in a chair, and say, "Muriel, whatcha doing hanging up there on the wall?" has to be given honorable mention.

HEART ATTACK

The Little Foxes (1941). Only the hard-hearted Bette Davis could steal a heart attack scene from the man (Herbert Marshall) who is actually having one. When Marshall is having his heart attack, the bottle of medicine drops from his hands and he pleads with Davis to get the other bottle from his room upstairs. Davis doesn't move from her chair. Director William Wyler, no dummy, keeps the camera on Davis's face while poor Marshall, in the background, is struggling to climb the stairs to get the other bottle. Only when Marshall collapses does she call for help.

On condition of anonymity, one heart attack scene fan revealed he was sure that if this ever happened to him, his wife would act the same way.

Something's Gotta Give (2003). On a lighter heart attack scene note, Jack Nicholson's heart attack in this movie won the club's membership vote because he wouldn't admit to taking Viagra until Keanu Reeves told him that if he did take Viagra, that could make the nitroglycerine drip in his arm fatal. Nicholson ripping the IV out of his arm always gets a laugh. Viagra fans wanted this scene for their own, but the D.O.A. quickly dismissed their motion before it got to trial.

Dr. Zhivago (1965). Doctor/poets who are fans of heart attack scenes know that the walls of Omar Sharif's heart are paper thin. He must have known he was dying. But when Sharif sees Julie Christie walking down that Moscow street, he hops off the tram and runs after her. The rest is heart attack movie history.

Meet Joe Black (1998). All they see is Anthony Hopkins have a heart attack warning. But heart attack fans understand that a star like Hopkins has to stick around until the Angel of Death (Brad Pitt) acquires a taste for peanut butter. Grateful for the guided tour of earthly life, Pitt gently leads Hopkins off the stage during a black-tie party at his luxurious mansion. Though cheated of Hopkins's final heart attack, everyone in the club understands why Hopkins tells Pitt, "It's hard to let go, isn't it?"

Four Weddings and a Funeral (1994). There's only one thing left to do after drinking eight glasses of champagne and dancing a Scottish reel for half an hour. And that is to have a heart attack. The upside to Simon Callow's sad end is that if he hadn't had his heart attack, this film would have simply been called *Four Weddings*, and his recipe for Duck à la Banana would not have been buried with him.

HITCHHIKING

Five Easy Pieces (1970). It was hard for the members to include a hitch-hiking scene that shows hitchhikers in such a bad light. Perhaps the worst hitchhiker in film history is Palm Apodaca, one of the lesbians to whom Jack Nicholson gives a lift. Apodaca talks about how filthy humans are for the whole trip: "Animals are not like that. They're always cleaning themselves. Did you ever see, umm ... pigeons? Well, he's always picking on himself and his friends. They're always picking bugs out of their hair all the time. Monkeys too. Except they do something out in the open that I don't go for." After a few hours of listening to this crap, Nicholson drops the two women off at the side of the road. The experience was not lost on Nicholson. In the final scene of the movie he stops at a gas station and dumps Karen Black by leaving her in the car and telling her he's going to get a candy bar. Then he hitches a ride

Hitchhiking fans never watch love scenes. All they watch is the end of *Five Easy Pieces* (1970) when Jack Nicholson leaves Karen Black in the car at a gas station and hitches a ride on a truck going to Alaska.

on a truck going to Alaska. He's so polite that the truck driver even lends him a warm coat.

It Happened One Night (1934). If you're planning to thumb a ride anywhere soon, don't listen to Clark Gable's advice on the position of your thumb. Just do what Claudette Colbert does. Lift your skirt up over your leg and the first car that passes will stop.

Monster (2003). Hitchhiking fans know not to stop for roadside hookers, especially if the hitcher happens to be Charlize Theron. Instead of sex, what you'll get is robbed and killed. After the release of this film, there was a big drop in the number of drivers who stop for hitchhikers. Hitchhikers should also be warned not stop at a roadside cafe run by Bette Davis. In *Petrified Forest* (1936), Duke Mantee was waiting there and Leslie Howard never made it out of the movie alive.

Wild Strawberries (1957). Hitchhiking fans have a particular soft spot for Victor Sjöström as the old widower who picks up three young students, two men and a woman, who help him recognize that he has become an embittered old man. By the end of the film, the young trio have helped to give him a sense of peace.

Two other actors held in high regard by hitchhiking movie nuts are Pee-Wee Herman, who hitchhiked his way across the country looking for his stolen bicycle, and Art Carney, who traveled throughout the country with his cat in *Harry and Tonto* (1974). Along the way Carney picked up a Bible-quoting hitchhiker and a 16-year-old runaway; his choice in hitchhikers was so good that it won him an Academy Award for Best Actor.

HITLER

Indiana Jones and the Last Crusade (1989). There's a nice little throwaway Hitler scene in this film that occurs when Indiana (Harrison Ford) and his father Henry (Sean Connery) travel to Berlin to get back the diary containing clues on the Holy Grail, which Hitler (Michael Sheard) wants for himself. The trip leads them to a Nazi book-burning rally in Berlin, where Indiana Jones bumps into the Führer himself. The scene is both loopy and ironic because Hitler does not realize he has met Indy or that he is actually holding the Grail Diary. Hitler then proceeds to casually open the diary to a random page, sign his name, and give it back to Indy.

Euro Trip (2004). Further proof of how much Hitler scene movie nuts love throwaway humor is their choice of this scene. A little German boy (Adam Dotlacil) is playing on the carpet while the two leads (Scott Mechlowicz and Jacob Pitts) are talking to his father. The kid pencils a Hitler mustache under his nose, gives Mechlowicz a "Heil Hitler" salute and starts goose-stepping around the living room. It's interesting to note that many Hitler scene fans believe the origin of that salute goes back to 1841, when the ballet *Giselle* was first performed. In the first act, Giselle a beautiful peasant girl, is trying to get Albrecht to dance with her when he puts out his right hand, palm out, turns his head and takes a step back. In ballet, this pantomime means "don't bug me," which is the emotion Germans may have been conveying whenever they gave Hitler the salute.

Manhunt (1941). When British big-game hunter Captain Alan Thorndike (Walter Pidgeon) slips through the forest undetected near the Berghof, Adolf Hitler's residence near Berchtesgarden, getting the dictator in his sights, he pulls the trigger on his unloaded rifle and gives a wave. He ponders a moment, then loads a live round, but is discovered at the last second by a guard and the shot goes wild. We only see Hitler for a brief second, but for Hitler scene fans length of Hitler screen time is no big deal.

The Producers (1968). Not many people know it but the Führer was terrific dancer. Only Mel Brooks could think of a line like that. Or others like "Don't be stupid. Be a smarty. Come and join the Nazi Party," some of the lyrics in the show *Springtime for Hitler*. The scene Hitler fans can't get enough of is when Zero Mostel and Gene Wilder are casting for the role of Hitler. The scene begins when the director says, "Will the dancing Hitlers please wait in the wings? We are only seeing singing Hitlers." They particularly like a guy dressed like Kaiser Wilhelm who sings "Have you ever heard a Deutsche band, mit a bang, mit a boom, mit a bang, bang — The poor guy never gets the last boom out because Mostel says, "Next!" A close second choice is the nasal tenor who sings, "A wandering minstrel I." Mel Brooks would get a kick out of my own Hitler story. When my nine-year-old son was asked by a teacher to write a composition about one of his parents, he began it with these words: "My father was Hitler's best friend. They hunted together in the Black Forest." I dined on that one for years.

Inglourious Basterds (2009). Brooks, an honorary member of the Hitler scene fan club, would probably also love the moment when Hitler, who is watching one of Himmler's propaganda movies, steps out into the lobby and asks the guard at the door if he has any gum.

HORSEPLAYER

Key Largo (1948). Though most movie fans think Claire Trevor won her Best Supporting Actress Academy Award for being a lush, they are mistaken.

Horseplayer scene fans continue to insist that Claire Trevor (standing, Lauren Bacall is seated) won her Best Supporting Actress Academy Award for the way she explained to Humphrey Bogart how she handicaps horses in *Key Largo* (1948).

According to members of the best horseplayer scenes fan club, Trevor won her award for the scene at the hotel's bar when she explains to Humphrey Bogart how she handicaps horses.

The Rocking Horse Winner (1949). Based on a story by D.H. Lawrence, this film about a rocking horse that can predict the winners of horse races may be disturbing to kids but not to horseplayers. Paul Grahame (John Howard Davies) rides his handicapping rocking horse so he and his butler (John Mills) can help his mother (Valerie Hobson) out of financial difficulty. The eerie shots of Davies on the rocking horse are pretty scary but not scary enough to prevent horseplayer fans from voting it onto their list by a margin of at least three lengths.

National Velvet (1944). Though Donald Crisp performed in more than 100 films, this was the only one he made a bet in. His horse won at big odds, but was disqualified because it was discovered that Elizabeth Taylor, the 12-year-old jockey who rode the horse, was a girl. But Taylor's eight husbands already knew that.

HUNCHBACK

The Name of the Rose (1986). Out of all the great hunchback scenes in movie history, the members of the hunchback scene fan club put this one at the top of their list. To a hunchback scene movie nut, Ron Perlman, the demented hunchback who speaks gibberish, is a hero. The scene that does it for them is the one in which Perlman is tied to the stake for burning, when he slyly starts blowing at the approaching flames and laughing to himself, knowing he can't possibly put them out. A brilliant piece of acting, even better than his portrayal of a good-guy demonic beast in *Hellboy* (2004).

The Hunchback of Notre Dame (1939). A vocal minority thought Charles Laughton's magnificent rescue of Maureen O'Hara from the hangman's scaffold was better than the way Ron Perlman faced being burned at the stake. But, alas, even Laughton's stirring cry of "Sanctuary!" made with his tongue lolling to one side of his mouth did not change the final vote.

Richard III (1955). The wicked and deformed Laurence Olivier's performance barely managed to finish a distant third in the vote. There were just too many hunchback fans who couldn't vote for a hunchback who murdered the little princes in the Tower of London.

INFIDELITY

Author's note: The infidelity scene fan club takes no responsibility for the inordinately large number of infidelity scenes listed, nor do the scenes reflect the morality of its members.

The Graduate (1967). Mrs. Robinson (Anne Bancroft) has obviously done this before. In fact, if it weren't for her perfect instructions, Dustin Hoffman wouldn't even know how to get a hotel room. It is Hoffman's insistence on having some conversation before they do it that almost leads to Bancroft walking out

In *The Graduate* (1967), Katharine Ross became the only actress in film history to get a marriage proposal while she was getting married (Brian Avery, right).

on him. But he does discover that the forty-year-old Mrs. Robinson was an art history major in college. The affair ends badly, as all movie fans know. Hoffman falls in love with Mrs. Robinson's daughter, Katharine Ross, breaking up her wedding at the last moment and riding off with Ross on a bus to nowhere.

The Descendants (2011). To show what they really think of infidelity in marriage, infidelity scene fans point to their admiration for a film that puts George Clooney's cheating wife into an irreversible coma. Had Clooney's wife not gone into a coma, his daughter would never have told him that her mother was having an affair with a real estate agent and Clooney would never have had another reason not to sell the family land to the developer who would have given the real estate agent who made him a cuckold a big commission. Better still, the movie would never have received five Academy Award nominations, including Best Picture, Best Director and Best Actor for Clooney.

Double Indemnity (1944). Before he going on to invent flubber in *The Absent-Minded Professor* (1961), Fred MacMurray sleeps with Barbara Stanwyck and helps her murder her husband. But when he finds out that Stanwyck is a serial cheater, she shoots him. Infidelity movie nuts don't like it when she can't fire the second shot to kill MacMurray because she discovers that she loves him. But it turns out all right for the members who like cheaters to pay for what they do, because MacMurray takes her gun and shoots her. Bleeding to death in the final scene, MacMurray tells his buddy Edward G. Robinson that the reason Robinson couldn't figure this one out was because the guy he was looking for was "too close." Right across the desk from him, in fact. Robinson lets MacMurray know that he was "closer than that." MacMurray replies, "I love you, too." Which proves that there's no infidelity between friends.

Freaks (1931). The lesson in this horror classic from Todd Browning is that beautiful circus trapeze artists who marry rich midgets for their money should never be unfaithful to them. Olga Baclanova finds this out when the freaks discover she not only cheated on her midget husband (Harry Earles) but also tried to poison him. They scare her witless and turn her into a sideshow chicken, which goes to show that when the freaks chanted, "Gobble. Gobble. One of us," they were being pretty prophetic.

Before he invented flubber, Fred MacMurray (right) had an affair with Barbara Stanwyck, who sweet-talked him into murdering her husband played by Tom Powers (center) in *Double Indemnity* (1944).

Wonder Boys (2000). The infidelity scenes in this under-appreciated film are a lot easier to take. That's because Frances McDormand and Michael Douglas are a lot easier to root for. McDormand is married to a jerk (Richard Thomas), and we never get to see Douglas's wife at all. And despite the Hays Office it all ends well. McDormand leaves Thomas, marries Douglas and has his baby As for Douglas, he trashes the 2,500-word book he can't stop writing and starts another.

The World of Henry Orient (1964). Infidelity scene enthusiasts aren't big fans of Tippy Walker and Merrie Spaeth. Had it not been for these two private school girls stalking him, concert pianist Peter Sellers would certainly have seduced the married Paula Prentiss. But they are rewarded later in this charming film when Sellers makes it with Angela Lansbury, a long-time favorite of infidelity fans ever since her affair with Charles Boyer in *Gaslight* (1944).

The Letter (1940). We never see Bette Davis being unfaithful to Herbert Marshall with Gale Sondergaard's husband. We only see Davis shoot the guy she committed infidelity with six times. Then there are all those clouds passing over the moon. All this happens at the beginning of the movie. But infidelity nuts know that the poor guy didn't try to rape her. We know because she wrote a letter pleading with her lover to visit her. Also, after she is acquitted of the murder, she tells Marshall, "With all my heart, I still love the man I killed!" When Davis walks out into the garden, there are more clouds passing over the moon. That's where the vengeful Sondergaard is waiting for her. The two women silently stare at each other. Then, as another cloud passes over the moon, Sondergaard stabs her.

Though most movie aficionados believe that Sondergaard killed Davis because she murdered her husband, there are more than a few infidelity movie nuts who have a different take on it. They believe that Sondergaard stabbed Davis because Davis's remarks about Sondergaard's "hideous chalky face; those eyes like a cobra's eyes" got back to her. The one thing everyone agrees on is to never invite Bette Davis and Gale Sondergaard to the same party.

Now, Voyager (1942). Infidelity fans know not to ask for the moon when they have the stars. So they are satisfied with the five days Bette Davis spends with the married Paul Henreid in Rio de Janeiro. They also like the way infidelity transforms Davis from an unattractive, overweight and repressed spinster into a beautiful woman.

Brief Encounter (1945). Scratch an infidelity aficionado and you will often find a romantic. This is why the unconsummated love affair between two married London suburbanites was put on the list. The fact that the final goodbye between Celia Johnson and Trevor Howard at the railway station snack bar is spoiled by the constant chattering of an acquaintance of Johnson's is enough of a punishment to soften the hearts of the members who had wished the two lovers could have found a way to consummate their relationship. Before adjourning, the membership always plays the Rachmaninoff piano concerto that recurs on the soundtrack throughout the film.

Citizen Kane (1941). "I run a couple of newspapers, what do you do?" may not be the greatest pick-up line, but it worked for Orson Welles on

Dorothy Comingore. Better he had kept his mouth shut. Their affair cost him the race for governor, Ruth Warrick divorced him and he ended up dying in an unfinished mansion with a lot of marble statues, pining for a sled he had when he was a kid.

Dr. Zhivago (1965). Okay, Omar Sharif was unfaithful to his wife while she was pregnant, but even the most hardened member of the Infidelity Scene Morals committee was moved when Sharif spotted his lover (Julie Christie) from the tram window and died of a heart attack while trying to reach her. In an informal poll of the membership, nearly everyone agreed that Rita Tushingham was Julie Christie's daughter and that Omar Sharif was her father.

American Beauty (1999). Embarrassed by the noisy way Annette Bening cheated on Kevin Spacey in that motel room with real estate mogul Peter Gallagher, members of the infidelity scene in fan club offered this recipe by way of an apology.

CHEATER'S CORN ON THE COB WITH SHALLOT BUTTER

INGREDIENTS
6 ears of corn
6 tbsp of butter
6 shallots

Peel back the husks from the corn but do not remove them. Do remove the silk. Spread each ear with shallot butter, which is made by lightly sautéing the chopped shallots in olive oil and butter, then mixing the shallots with fresh butter in a blender. Rewrap each ear of corn in its husk and then wrap in aluminum foil. Grill the corn over the barbecue for about half an hour, turning every five minutes.

A special cheater's forgiveness award was given to John Garfield for not sleeping with Marie Windsor, his partner's wife, in *Force of Evil* (1948). The award wipes the slate clean, letting Garfield off the hook for his affairs with Joan Crawford in *Humoresque* (1946) and Lana Turner in *The Postman Always Rings Twice* (1946), in which both actresses wind up dead. Garfield beat out George Clooney by three votes. Though Clooney's performance in *Up in the*

Air (2009) was flawless, many felt he was beaten because he didn't know Vera Farmiga was married until the end of the film.

INVITATION REFUSAL

The Razor's Edge (1957). The actor whom invitation refusal scene fans regard as the doyen of invitation refusers is Clifton Webb. In this pre–Bill Murray version of the Somerset Maugham novel, Webb puts so much effort into his refusal of an invitation to the Riviera "A-list" party of the year that it literally kills him. Admirers of the scene still remember the tactfully worded letter of regret dictated to Tyrone Power in which Webb says he is "unable to attend because of a previous appointment with his maker." They are his last words.

The irony that Webb had not actually been invited to the party and that Power had to steal the invitation was not lost on invitation refusal scene experts. But it did not dampen their admiration of Webb's ultimate sacrifice to the genre.

The Egyptian (1954). The only known case of a film actor who offers an invitation *and* refuses its acceptance is pulled off by Bella Darvi. Darvi, a popular courtesan in ancient Egypt, promises Edmond Purdom, a young ancient Egyptian medical student, that she will show him perfection in love. When Purdom accepts the invitation, first hocking his parents' prepayment to the embalmers of the House of the Dead in order to raise money for her fee, Darvi refuses to accept Purdom's acceptance of her invitation. To be fair, Darvi claims that by refusing to go to bed with Purdom, she *is* showing him perfection in love. Invitation refusal fans didn't buy that at all and voted the scene into the refusal category unanimously. As for Purdom, he spends the next seven years working in the House of the Dead to pay for his parents' funeral.

The Godfather (1972). Jack Woltz must have been really sorry he refused Vito Corleone's invitation to give Johnny Fontane a part in his next movie, given that because the next day he woke up in bed with the severed head of his prized racehorse. A great scene, yes, but nasty to watch.

JOB INTERVIEW

American Beauty (1999). A job interview scene that is foreshadowed by a guy quitting his job, telling his boss to go fuck himself, and then blackmailing him for almost sixty thousand dollars is something worth waiting for. So when the manager of Mr. Smiley, a fast food drive-through, tells Kevin Spacey that his experience is twenty years old, Spacey knows how to deliver just the right deadpan response: "Well, I'm sure there have been amazing technological advances in the industry, but surely you must have some sort of training program. It seems unfair to presume I won't be able to learn." Spacey not only gets the job but is also able to serve his wife (Annette Bening) a burger and fries when she drives up with the sleazeball she has just had a quickie with at a nearby motel.

Kramer vs. Kramer (1979). Dustin Hoffman also knows his way around a job interview. When he needs a job right away so he can keep custody of his son, he tells the interviewer, "This is a one-day offer. You saw my book, you know I can handle the work. You're gonna have to let me know today, not at the end of the holidays. If you want me, make a decision right now."

Taxi Driver (1976). Robert De Niro found the interview to get his job driving a cab to be a lot easier. The interview only lasted about a minute. The dispatcher asks him, "Wanna work uptown nights? South Bronx? Harlem?" De Niro replies, "I'll work anytime, anywhere." The next question was even easier, especially if you're an actor named De Niro who's playing a character named Travis Bickle: "Will you work Jewish holidays?"

The Man in the Gray Flannel Suit (1956). Nobody could blame Gregory Peck for being pissed off when he is interviewed for a job at the television network owned by Fredric March. Arthur O'Connell, the actor doing the interview, is lying back in his chair/bed behind his desk while he asks Peck a few questions. Peck can't even see him. O'Connell explains that he does this because his doctor wants him to relax more. Then Peck is told to go into a room and finish this sentence: The most significant thing about me is..." Peck goes into an office, puts some paper into the typewriter and stares at it. This gives the director a nice chance to show a few flashbacks of Peck's war years. When the flashbacks are over, Peck types a short paragraph that says, "The most significant thing about me is that I am applying for a job here." Thanks to Peck's star appeal, and the fact that he reminds March of his son who was killed in the war, he lands the job.

Up in the Air (2009). Anna Kendrick graduated at the top of her class and could have had her pick of jobs, yet she chose to travel to Omaha to take a job firing people. When asked why by a prospective employer, she replied, "I followed a boy." She got the job, mainly because George Clooney told Kendrick's interviewer that hiring her would be the best decision he ever made.

LAUGHING

Quest for Fire (1982). Technical advisors in the caveman laughter sub-genre have been advising Hollywood moviemakers to delete laughing scenes from caveman movies for decades. Victor Mature didn't laugh in *One Million B.C.*, Raquel Welch didn't laugh in the remake of *One Million B.C.*, and Trog didn't laugh in *Trog*. Because Jean-Jacques Annaud, the director of this French import, used no technical advisor, Rae Dawn Chong became the first caveperson to laugh on film. She laughs when one of the cavemen she is traveling with gets hit on the head by a rock. Her laughter is so catchy that soon all the cavemen are laughing, even the one who got hit. The resulting scene is the recipient of two thumbs up from Roger Ebert.

Sleeper (1973). A sentimental choice among laughing scene fans is the scene in which Diane Keaton passes the laughing orb around, causing her house robot (Woody Allen) to laugh, although Allen's laugh is actually more of a closed-mouthed snicker, as a full-on laugh would blow his cover. More than a few laughing scene fans who cast their ballot for this rare screen moment have confessed that they chose the scene because it is the only one that they can remember Woody Allen laughing in.

Crimes of the Heart (1986). When Jessica Lange comes back from an all-night date with Sam Shepard, she finds Diane Keaton and Sissy Spacek looking pretty glum because they just learned their grandfather is in a coma. So when Lange says she bets that Grandpa will go into a coma when he finds out what she's been up to, Spacek and Keaton start to laugh. And when they tell her that Grandpa is already in a coma, their laughter becomes near hysteria. Which just goes to show you how funny laughter is and how many different things there are to laugh about. Diane Keaton won the special notice of fans interested in laughing technique for the snort she perfected in this scene.

Sometimes a Great Notion (1971). Richard Jaeckel may be the only actor in movie history to drown laughing. Paul Newman, who starred in and directed this film about the dangers of laughing while underwater, made Jaeckel laugh while trying to give him air via mouth-to-mouth resuscitation when he was trapped by a fallen log. Jaeckel thought the idea of two grown men kissing underwater was funny. Drowning was the result. Except for a small group of laughing scene fans, few film buffs know about this singular laughing scene. This may be due to the fact that the film had two titles and two directors and also was not a great box office success. It is hoped that this award will remedy that situation.

The Pink Panther Strikes Again (1976). The endless questions are still being discussed in laughing scene fan circles: Is Herbert Lom laughing because he is trying to kill Peter Sellers? Is he laughing because the room is filled with laughing gas? Or is he laughing because Peter Sellers's fake nose is melting off? Being a very easygoing group, laughing scene fans are not inordinately concerned that they have not found the answers to these questions. Since the scene is definitely a laughing scene, and a very funny one indeed, it was voted in on merit alone.

Mary Poppins (1964). One of the most unusual laughing scene heroes in the movies is Ed Wynn, who played Uncle Albert in this magical Disney release. Wynn had the uncanny ability to rise into the air whenever he laughed. Laughing scene auditors report that Wynn did not use a double, nor were there any wires holding him up in the scene that won him this award. As for Dick Van Dyke and the two children, the wires were clearly visible. Of course, Mary Poppins (Julie Andrews) already knew how to fly.

Wynn was so adept at rising to the ceiling when he laughed that he often had tea there. It is not generally known, but it is the ambition of every laughing scene fan to master Wynn's special skill. Visitors to the laughing scene club-house have often reported hearing the song "I love to laugh, ha-ha-ha-ha!" coming from the "Laughing Room," where members test their laughing and their levitation. To date, no one has discovered Wynn's knack, though many have tried.

Kiss of Death (1947). Just when you thought Hollywood had run out of things to laugh at, along came this low-budget gangster film that cata-pulted Tommy Udo from a laughing scene cult hero into a star. Udo's high-pitched laughter as he pushed an old lady in a wheelchair down the stairs continues to thrill laughing scene enthusiasts to this day. In an effort to escape from being typecast as a killer who laughs when he does mean things to people, Tommy Udo changed his name to Richard Widmark. Laughing scene fans who have kept track of Udo's career as Richard Widmark have now and then been rewarded with a burst of award-caliber laughter from their hero.

Citizen Kane (1941). A small group of laughing scene fanatics still harbor the notion that if Dorothy Comingore hadn't laughed when Orson Welles got splashed by that puddle, Welles, and not Ronald Reagan, would have been the first president of the United States who had formerly been an actor. Their reasoning is not without merit. If Comingore hadn't laughed when she did then, Welles would never have heard her sing, he would never have begun the affair, and he never would have been caught by Big Jim Geddes. This last point cost Welles an election that could have been a stepping stone to the presidency.

Putting historical aspects aside, the scene is also something of a rarity, since it may be the only time in film history that an actress laughed while suffering from a toothache. This was the cause of some friction between dentist scene fans and laughing scene fans. It is not generally known, but some years after the film was released, dentist scene fans claimed this scene as their own. At a secret but well-attended meeting between the two groups, it was finally decided that the scene should remain in the "laughing scene" category. There were two overriding reasons: Welles was not a dentist, and Comingore's toothache mysteriously ended without treatment.

The actor most beloved by laughing scene fans is Edward Arnold, whose laugh, which sounded something like "gah ... geh-geh-geh," is often imitated at laughing scene fan get-togethers. (The laughing scene fan able to do the best Edward Arnold laugh imitation is reported to be Ted Williams, the head of a construction firm in New York.) Arnold's distinctive laugh graced such films as *I'm No Angel* (1933), *Cardinal Richelieu* (1935), *Man About Town* (1939), *The Devil and Daniel Webster* (1941), *Meet John Doe* (1941), and *Dear Ruth* (1947). Laughing scene fans report that it's a rare Edward Arnold film in which this laughing scene hero does not get in at least one "gah ... geh-geh-geh."

LIBRARY

Ghostbusters (1984). Talk about telekinetic activity. There are not only books flying off the shelves at the 42nd Street Main Public Library, but also stacks falling down and free-floating apparitions. So what question does Bill Murray ask the 60-year-old librarian who saw all this? He asks her if she is menstruating right now. Library scene fans suggest that the only possible excuse for this funny but dumb question is that this was the Ghostbusters' unofficial first job.

Atonement (2007). There's a good reason why the wives of library scene fans don't let their husbands watch the library scene in this overrated film. But those lucky enough to see it are treated to a sizzling lovemaking scene between Keira Knightley and James McAvoy.

The Name of the Rose (1986). Some of the books in the library in this remote abbey in northern Italy are not only pornographic, but can also kill you. It is a nonconformist monk played by Sean Connery who discovers the reason that several of the monks have died. The pages of the forbidden books were laced with poison, and the monks who licked their fingers to separate the pages ingested the poison and died. The final scene in the library has a spectacular fire that almost cooks Connery. In a 5-to-4 decision, the D.O.A. allowed these scenes to remain in the library scene category despite an intense public relations campaign by a determined group of poison scene fans.

All the President's Men (1976). It doesn't matter that Robert Redford and Dustin Hoffman, as *Washington Post* reporters Bob Woodward and Carl Bernstein, weren't checking out books but only trying to find out what books the White House had requested to check out. The scene set in the Main Reading Room of the Library of Congress helped win this film its place in library scene history. Redford and Hoffman are shown sitting at a desk, plowing through massive stacks of slips as the camera pans upward to the dome of the reading room, showing the vast expanse of the circular room and making everyone below look like distant specks.

The Thief (1952). The Library of Congress is also a great place for a nuclear physicist to hand over top secrets to the enemy. Ray Milland, sobered up from his role in *The Lost Weekend* (1945), probably still didn't feel up to remembering any lines of dialogue, so Russell Rouse, the film's director, was thoughtful enough to shoot the entire film without any dialogue at all. No spoken dialogue in an age of sound was a little ahead of its time and the movie didn't do so well. When French director Michel Hazanavicius tried this trick in 2011 with *The Artist*, it won an Academy Award for Best Picture and a Best Actor award for Jean Dujardin.

The Squid and the Whale (2005). Even after library sex, library poisoning, library ghosts, and library espionage, the library scene fan club felt they needed something more to demonstrate the importance of library scenes in film. The "something" turned out to be masturbation. In this funny but disturbing scene the eleven-year-old son of divorcing parents Laura Linney and Jeff Daniels gets up from his table, walks between the bookcases, takes out a pornographic photo and masturbates. Wiping off his sperm on the book jackets in the nearby shelves is the clincher.

MARCHING BAND

The founder of the marching band fan club is a Los Angeles screenwriter who, after a particularly unpleasant disappointment (the series he was hired to write an episode for was cancelled because the network hated the pilot), found himself in a park watching a choose-up football game. At halftime, the marching band was a ten-year-old kid marching across the football field while carrying a boombox that played "Stars and Stripes Forever." That night the disappointed screenwriter saw *Pretty Poison*, the movie that became the first marching band scene selection even before there was a marching band scene fan club.

Pretty Poison (1968). Fans of marching band movie scenes love it when a marching band scene opens the movie, and none is better than when Anthony Perkins spots Tuesday Weld leading her high school marching band. The club members agreed with their founder and voted it as number one on the list. The scene where Perkins keeps seeing the band when he looks at those little red bottles on the conveyer belt solidified the vote.

The Bridge on the River Kwai (1957). Another marching band scene that opens a movie is in this fine David Lean film starring Alec Guinness. The sight of a battalion of British POWs marching into that jungle POW camp while whistling the "Colonel Bogey March" is thrilling. Though mentioned in my earlier book solely as a whistling scene, I now include this movie in the best marching band category because at Japanese prisoner of war camps, there's always a full-fledged marching band that takes over on the soundtrack when the whistling stops.

Drumline (2002). Halftime is game time at Atlanta A&T in this movie about a college where it's the marching band that competes with other colleges, not the football team. What lifts this film into the award category is that the drummers have to do one-handed pushups and run up and down the stadium with their drums raised over their heads to stay in shape.

Take the Money and Run (1969). Virgil Starkwell may be the only member of a marching band to play the cello. But he has to supply his own chair. Only the eccentric Woody Allen could have come up with a marching band cellist in a film that the *New York Times* movie critic Vincent Canby accurately called a "feature-length, two-reel comedy."

Music Man (1962). When con man Professor Harold Hill (Robert Preston) comes to River City to sell trombones and then tells the high school marching band to learn to play via the "think system," a method in which they merely have to think of a tune over and over and will know how to play it without ever touching their instruments, you know there's a great marching band scene coming. The film delivers and it was seventy-six trombones that led the big parade, with a hundred and ten cornets close at hand.

From page 3 of *Cinema Paradiso*: Thanks to a recent renovation, the doorbell to the marching band clubhouse now plays "Stars and Stripes Forever" when you ring it. The idea was borrowed by the club members from the march Jimmy Stewart's doorbell plays in *Mr. Smith Goes to Washington* (1939).

MARRIAGE PROPOSAL

Little Women (1937). Yes, Paul Lukas actually used the phrase "dare I hope" in his charming proposal of marriage to Katharine Hepburn in the final scene of this delightfully old-fashioned film. Hepburn knew a great marriage proposal when she saw one. Though Lukas was older, poor and foreign, she accepted immediately. Of course, the rain was a nice touch. So was Lukas's transparent excuse of delivering the book. Apparently, when deciding whether to marry someone, hearing the words "dare I hope" counts for a lot. Marriage proposal scouts have been keeping a watchful eye out for this phrase ever since the release of this classic marriage proposal film. Unhappily, they cannot report ever hearing it used again.

It's a Wonderful Life (1946). Statistics from the marriage proposal scene fan club reveal that in the year this Frank Capra film was released, the number of marriages jumped 62 percent. What caused this unusual increase? Many feel it was Donna Reed's refusal to accept Jimmy Stewart's impassioned recital of all the reasons he didn't want to marry her. They theorize that women who saw this scene began to imitate Donna Reed whenever a suitor gave his reason for not wanting to get married, and that the large increase in marriages that year was an indication of how deeply this scene affected American women.

Even though it worked out okay for Reed and Stewart, some marriage counselors have linked this scene—and the marriages it caused—to the current high rate of divorce.

Three Strangers (1946). Admirers of marriage proposal scenes are an odd lot. They are not inclined to give much weight to the reasons for a proposal of marriage. This may explain the inclusion of Jerome K. Arbutney's proposal to one of his rich and widowed clients in this superb film noir starring Sydney Greenstreet, Peter Lorre and Geraldine Fitzgerald.

At one point in the scene, Arbutney, wonderfully played by Greenstreet, actually falls to his knees in his zeal to win the lady. Unfortunately, the widow (from whom Greenstreet has been stealing money) has been in touch with her dear departed husband, who told her to refuse the offer. This has always been a great disappointment to marriage proposal scene fans since it was the only marriage proposal Greenstreet ever made on screen. Notes from his secret diary confirm what many have long believed. It was this refusal that shattered Greenstreet's confidence and kept him a bachelor in every film he made afterward.

Mildred Pierce (1945). There are a fair number of actresses who have asked men to marry them in movies, but it takes a Joan Crawford to ask a man to ask her to marry him. That's just what Crawford does when she walks in on Zachary Scott after dumping him and proposes to him with the words, "Ask me to marry you." Of course, she is doing it for that arch-spoiled brat of films, her daughter Veda (Ann Blyth). No dummy, Scott proposes that Crawford give him one-third of her restaurant. Crawford wants Veda back and the price of that is getting Scott back, so she accepts his proposal, in addition to the proposal she proposed in the first place. Had either known what was in store for them, neither would have accepted either of the proposals.

The Hunchback of Notre Dame (1939). Probably the most unsentimental proposal of marriage in movie history was made by Maureen O'Hara, as Esmerelda, to Edmond O'Brien, who played Gringoire, in this Hollywood version of the Victor Hugo classic. When O'Hara sees O'Brien about to be hanged by Thomas Mitchell, the King of the Beggar's Union, she asks, "Are you going to hang that man?" "Unless you'll take him," Mitchell replies. "I'll take him," says O'Hara. Surprisingly, this three-word proposal of marriage struck a responsive chord in the heart of every marriage proposal fan who saw it. The question that still haunts them, however, is this: would Maureen O'Hara have made the same proposal if she had known what was going to happen to Edmond O'Brien in *D.O.A.*?

Crossing Delancey (1988). Before revealing the reason for including this marriage scene in the awards category, three basic marriage proposal rules should be explained: (1) Whether a proposal is accepted is of no importance to the judging panel. (2) The proposal need not be made by the person who wants to get married. (3) It can be made in the presence of others.

Applying these rules to this film we find that, yes, there were other people present besides Peter Riegart and Amy Irving, the woman he loves. Yes, that was Sylvia Miles who actually made the proposal for Riegart. And, yes, Amy Irving refused the proposal. The panel was free to disregard these facts. What they did regard was the fact that Sylvia Miles was eating pickles with her pot roast while she proposed to Irving. Considering that Peter Riegart was in the pickle business, this showed great delicacy of feeling to her client (Riegart) and it was this fact that earned the scene its rightful place in the marriage proposal hall of fame.

Rebecca (1940). One of the truly great marriage proposals in screen history involves a social blunder by the normally correct Sir Laurence Olivier that is compounded by a misunderstanding from the normally sharp-witted Florence Bates. This rare marriage proposal double faux pas occurs when Maxim De Winter, intending to ask Rebecca to be his wife, mistakes Florence Bates for Joan Fontaine, especially in her dealings with Mrs. Danvers (Judith Anderson). Many marriage proposal scene fans feel that Olivier would have been better off marrying Bates, who would have been more of a match for the cruel Mrs. Danvers.

Rocky II (1979). The only marriage proposal in film history made with a tiger as a witness takes place when Rocky proposes to Adrian during a trip to the zoo on a snowy winter day. His words aren't particularly romantic. Adrian doesn't hear him at first and Rocky has to lift her ear muffs to re-propose (a nice touch). What he said was this: "I was wondering if you wouldn't mind marrying me very much." Her acceptance is equally low-key:

"Yes, I'd like to marry you." Rocky is so overjoyed that he invites the tiger to the wedding.

Carnal Knowledge (1971). When Ann-Margret sat on that unmade bed trying to put on her makeup and said to Jack Nicholson, "I want to get married," marriage proposal scene fans in the audience wept openly. "It's a very depressing scene," one fan commented after he regained his composure. "Yes, it is," clarified his female companion. "She ends up married to that creep!" It was these differing perceptions of the character Nicholson played that resulted in a curtailment of any discussion of the film after the final vote. Though the male members recognized that Nicholson's attitude toward women wasn't very nice, they couldn't go along when the female members kept referring to him as "the biggest prick in film history."

The Graduate (1967). Is it possible to get a proposal of marriage while you are at the altar getting married to another man? Yes, reports Katharine Ross, who got one just like that from Dustin Hoffman during the wacky denouement of this very popular release directed by Mike Nichols. All Hoffman had to do was shout her name, whisk her out of the church and get her into the back of a bus. To answer the many fans who have wondered if a marriage with that kind of beginning could work out, the answer is no. Ross was spotted out west two years later, first as a school teacher and then when she took up with Butch Cassidy and the Sundance Kid.

MEMORY

Cheers for Miss Bishop (1941). No one in the memory scene fan club remembered why they left the Rosemary DeCamp memory scene out, so in a rare emergency session they rectified their error. In a unanimous vote they placed it right behind the scene in *Citizen Kane* (1941) in which Everett Sloane said he still remembered the girl he saw for just a moment 50 years ago. In this long forgotten memory scene, DeCamp, one of Martha Scott's students at Midwestern College, is accused of cheating on an exam. Her teacher thinks she brought the textbook into the examination room because her answers were taken word for word from the book. To prove her innocence, Scott has DeCamp recite the entire Declaration of Independence from memory. The examining board is amazed at her perfect recollection and realizes that DeCamp has a photographic memory and didn't cheat after all. DeCamp is so happy she asks them if they want her to recite the Constitution, too. Another nice touch occurs at the end of the film, when DeCamp's photographic memory has helped her become a world-famous librarian.

The Treasure of the Sierra Madre (1948). Alfonso Bedoya is the victim of a Mexican boy's good memory in this John Huston masterpiece. Though few memory scene fans have shown much interest in the first two hours of this classic tale of greed and memory, all snap to attention during the final five minutes. That's when the little Mexican boy lifts the saddle cloths of the mules Bedoya is trying to sell. It's a thrilling moment. If the kid hadn't remembered they were the same mules he sold to the late Fred C. Dobbs, Bedoya would still be alive today. But he always remembers. Memory scene fans, not known for their sensitivity to the fate of Mexican bandits, would have it no other way.

Citizen Kane (1941). No, Everett Sloane didn't remember who or what "Rosebud" was, but he did remember a girl he saw on a ferry 50 years earlier. "She was wearing a white dress. I only saw her for a few seconds. She didn't see me at all," Sloane told the reporter. "Yet, I'll bet there hasn't been a day when I haven't thought about that girl," he added wistfully.

Sloane's extraordinary feat of memory, added to the fact that he was still in love with the girl in the white dress, weighed heavily with memory scene fans. It is not a scene one can easily forget, and few seeing this film gem fail to share Sloane's regret at not meeting the girl, which is another reason memory scene fans decided to confer yet another movie scene award to this extraordinary, still fresh Orson Welles masterpiece.

The 39 Steps (1935). Even as a young director, Alfred Hitchcock knew where to begin and end his films. The result is a pair of memory scenes that fans rank as "unforgettable." This unusually high assessment is due to a character in the film called Mr. Memory, who is, indeed, "one of the most remarkable men in the world."

In the opening scene Mr. Memory answers a number of pretty good questions, including a rather dull one from Robert Donat about how far Winnipeg is from Montreal. Donat's question in the final scene is not quite so dull. About to be arrested, he asks Mr. Memory, "What are the 39 steps?"

Mr. Memory gets as far as saying, "The 39 steps are a secret organization of spies in the British government —" when a shot rings out and kills the poor man. But he doesn't die until he clears Donat by revealing the secret plans he had memorized.

One interesting side note to this film is that it contains a scene that may be the first time a scream turns into a train whistle. It occurs when Donat's landlady discovers the body of the murdered spy in his flat. In the middle of her scream, Hitchcock cuts to the Flying Scotsman speeding to Scotland, its whistle blaring. (This information is printed with the permission of the train scene fan club, whose president shamefacedly admits that he lost the rights to this scene when he bet into a one-card draw at the weekly memory scene fan club poker game.)

Letter from an Unknown Woman (1948). It is not Louis Jourdan but his mute manservant who remembers Jourdan's affair with Joan Fontaine. Jourdan, now a dissolute concert pianist, has been up all night reading the letter that tells him how much Fontaine loved him and how she bore him a son and how they both died of fever. He learns all this on the morning that he is to fight a duel with a jealous husband whose wife he has been having an affair with.

Memory scene fans, who never stay past the moment Jourdan remembers who Joan Fontaine is, voted the scene into film history without knowing whether Jourdan survives the duel. Not being a memory scene fan myself, I have seen the ending and would like to inform them that he does not.

Gigi (1958). It had never been tried before — a song about memory in an award-winning memory scene. When Hermione Gingold and Maurice Chevalier first sang the captivating Lerner and Loewe classic, "I Remember It Well," memory scene fans were so charmed they made it the permanent theme song of their annual dinner dance. Fan club members meet for the black-tie affair each year promptly at nine (or is it eight?). They are always on time (though many are late?). A tenor sings (or is it a baritone?). Are they getting old? Oh, no, not them! Ah yes, they remember it well.

Finding Nemo (2003). No one in the memory scene fan club can remember ever considering an animated film for its award before. But this film they will remember because one of its characters is a fish with short-term memory loss. First the fish, named Dory, tells Marlin, another fish, that she has seen the ship that captured Nemo, Marlin's son, and then tells Marlin to follow her. After a frantic underwater swim, Dory suddenly stops to ask Marlin why he is following her. The rest is memory scene history, proving that a scene that features a fish who suffers from short-term memory loss ranks pretty high with memory scene movie nuts.

MEN'S ROOM

The seriousness of the meeting to choose the best men's room scene in film history began on a light note. The president of the club told of his experience at a Brooklyn multiplex when, after seeing *Midnight in Paris*, he was heading for the men's room. Following the directional arrows leading him to where he wanted to go, he found two doors. One door read, "MEN"; the other read, "X-MEN." After a moment of polite laughter, the vote for the best men's room scene was taken.

True Lies (1994). Arnold Schwarzenegger may have taken the longest men's room pee in movie history. But the result was a spectacular shoot-out where three terrorists who followed him into the men's room were shot. The old guy sitting in the stall as all this was going on was lucky. He didn't get a scratch.

12 O'Clock High (1949)/*Mr. Smith Goes to Washington* (1939). Rare, but not unheard of, is a dead heat in men's room scenes. Rarer still are awards to scenes about men's rooms that do not even show a men's room. The former film just needed one line uttered by Gregory Peck to qualify, the one in which he angrily tells Richard Carlson, "If there's a navigator who can't find the men's room, you get him. Because you rate him." The other won its award on the strength of a line by Eugene Palette after they lose Jimmy Stewart in the Washington, D.C., train station: "Did you look in the...?" And the actor looking for Stewart says, "Yeah." The beauty of this exchange is that the men's room doesn't even have to be mentioned.

Patton (1970). The Academy Awards may have saluted this movie with eight richly deserved Oscars, but the membership of the men's room fan club were bitterly disappointed that it wasn't nine. To a man, they believe that if the Academy had an award for this category, the scene in the Algerian men's room between General Montgomery and General Bedell Smith would have won hands down. First, while Bedell Smith is at the urinal, Montgomery fogs up the mirror and outlines his plan of attack. Then, as they leave, he remarks to Bedell Smith how ironic it is that the plans for the Allied attack on Sicily would have been drawn up in an Algerian men's room.

Pulp Fiction (1994). The putz should never have come out of the bathroom. Hiding there with a mean-looking pistol while Samuel L. Jackson and John Travolta are murdering his pals, he spends most of the scene in the bathroom while trying to screw up his courage to come out. When he does come out blasting at Jackson and Travolta, he misses with all six shots. After the two hit men recover from the shock of a wild man coming out of the bathroom and shooting at them, they calmly shoot him down. Many men's room scene fans swear they could hear the poor guy mutter a self-deprecating "schmuck" as he lay dying.

The Social Network (2010). Not since Bob Balaban gave Jon Voight oral sex in a movie theater men's room in the 1969 film *Midnight Cowboy* has sex in a men's room been tried. Mark Zuckerberg and Eduardo Saverin were the lucky guys this time. It all happens in the stall of a public restroom after they create Facebook. We only see Saverin's feet but the audience knows what's happening because at the end of the encounter Saverin tells Zuckerberg, "We got groupies." That both films won Academy Awards for Best Picture and Best Director is not lost on men's room movie fans.

Psycho (1960). The bathroom of Janet Leigh's room at the Bates Motel can't exactly be called a men's room, but it is so iconic that men's room scene fans allowed it to be considered as a non-voting entry. It should be noted that fainthearted members who don't like to watch a beautiful woman being stabbed to death in a shower prefer to watch Mel Brooks being stabbed to death with a newspaper by the bellboy while he takes a shower. In this very funny scene from *High Anxiety* (1977), it's not blood that runs down the drain. It's newspaper ink.

MINE CAVE-IN

The Treasure of the Sierra Madre (1948). Cave-in scene fans have a special fondness for cave-ins in which a movie score lets them know that a character is going into a collapsed gold mine to rescue the guy who is going to shoot him later on in the movie. So when those timber supports conk Humphrey Bogart on the head, and Tim Holt sees the dust coming out of the mine entrance, we know he's going in there to pull Bogart out because the music tells us he will.

Zorba the Greek (1964). When they hear the crack of timber and see the dust pouring out of that lignite mine on Crete, cave-in scene movie nuts know that Anthony Quinn isn't going to let them down. He doesn't. He walks out of the mine, gives the miners who were afraid to go in a withering glance and says, "What?" Quinn lost out to Rex Harrison for the Best Actor Oscar that year, but his sharp rebuke in that wonderful scene has been used by movie aficionados for over fifty years whenever they wish to express annoyance.

The Big Carnival (1951). Members of the cave-in scene fan club let out a collective sigh of relief when the 33 Chilean miners were safely rescued. Their relief was not only for the miners, but also for themselves. The membership had written letters to all the drilling companies involved in the rescue, telling them not to drill from the top. They suspected that Kirk Douglas was up to his old tricks and that drilling this way would only prolong the operation so Douglas could win a Pulitzer. That's what he did in this movie and the poor guy trapped in the mine died. Luckily, none of the drillers had seen the movie, sometimes called *Ace in the Hole*, and the letters from cave-in scene fans were filed in the loony bin. The members did receive an angry letter from Douglas, who said he has never been to Chile.

How Green Was My Valley (1941). It's not dust that tells everyone in a Welsh mining town that there's been a cave-in. It's a warning whistle. This time it catches the attention of Sara Allgood. Veteran mine disaster fans know that this means it's Donald Crisp who won't make it out of the mine alive. That final scene, with Roddy McDowall crawling through the collapsed timbers to find his dying father and then cradling Crisp's head in his lap as they come up from the mine, is truly heartbreaking. Mine cave-in aficionados take solace in the fact that Crisp didn't die in vain. He won an Oscar for Best Supporting Actor for his role in this film and lived to act in numerous other films in the subsequent years.

MIRROR

American Psycho (2000). Christian Bale's narcissistic mirror performance as he flexes, poses and mugs gets high marks from the mirror scene fan club. Had it not been for the members of the psychiatrist scene fan club who share their clubhouse and sometimes attend meetings, mirror scene movie nuts would never have known that all those grisly axe and chain saw murders were only imagined by Bale. However, there are some members who continue to believe that the murders were real. The question is still being discussed.

Ruthless (1945). The mirror scene in this nearly forgotten masterpiece is a longtime favorite of mirror scene fans. The mirror is used for one reason and one reason only—to let Sydney Greenstreet know that his beautiful wife doesn't love him. Greenstreet is a good sport about it all. When his wife pushes him in front of their cheval glass and tells him in a very nasty manner, "You want to know why I don't love you? Look! Look at yourself," he just looks at his reflection and laughs: "A-heh ... a-heh ... a-heh-heh-heh." It is a particularly Greenstreetian laugh and the director gets the most out of the scene by shooting Greenstreet's reflection in the mirror at an upward angle from the floor.

Taxi Driver (1976). Robert De Niro's masterful portrayal of a man who thinks his mirror is talking to him won out over its closest rival, the Wicked Queen talking to her mirror (*Snow White and the Seven Dwarfs*, 1937), by one vote. Everyone was bitterly disappointed that both scenes could not be listed, but the Mirror Scene Rule Book clearly states that when more than one mirror scene involves someone asking a question of a mirror, only one can be chosen. "Mirror, mirror on the wall, who's the fairest of them all?" was judged to be a better question than "You talkin' to me?," but what finally tipped the scale in De Niro's favor was that he drew a gun on his mirror when it didn't answer him.

The Shining (1980). When Danny takes his mother's lipstick and writes "REDRUM" on the bedroom door, one can palpably feel the anticipation of mirror scene fans in the audience. The anticipation may be caused by the fact that a surprising number of them can read and write backward. In an unguarded moment, Arnold Zellermeyer once told me that they have often bored their friends at parties by showing off this skill. Boredom, however, is not Shelley Duvall's reaction when her son shows off his "mirror writing" skills in this scary and eccentric Kubrick thriller. Instead she nearly jumps out of her skin. To be fair, with Jack Nicholson downstairs getting nuttier by the minute, and seeing the word "REDRUM" reflecting in the mirror, who could blame her?

Dracula (1931). The brief, but sly mirror scene in this Bela Lugosi classic did not go unnoticed by mirror scene fans. The canny Van Helsing knows that Count Dracula would never walk into a room with a mirror prominently displayed, so he prepares a small box, which, when opened, has a mirror on the inside. When Lugosi is safely inside the room, Van Helsing opens the box and looks into the mirror to see if Lugosi's reflection is visible. Since vampires do not traditionally have a mirror reflection, he does not see Lugosi in the mirror.

When Van Helsing confronts Lugosi with the mirror, Bela knocks it out of his hand in a rare fit of vampire pique. Now Van Helsing knows for certain that Lugosi is a vampire, Lugosi knows that Van Helsing knows he is a vampire, and mirror scene fans know they can safely include a classic vampire mirror scene on their awards list.

Many film fans are under the assumption that the *Mirror Scene Rule Book* states a vampire mirror scene must be included in any list of awards. It does not. This film won its place on merit alone.

Broadcast News (1987). The height at which Holly Hunter's mirror was placed on her apartment wall has always been a source of great amusement among mirror scene fans. Not known for their senses of humor, they surprised members of the D.O.A. at their triannual awards dinner by laughing during the presentation of this award. When the scene in which Holly Hunter has to climb up on a chair in order to look at herself in the mirror for her date with William Hurt was shown on the monitor, a definite outbreak of giggling could be heard at the mirror scene fan club table. Their president, Bret Schlesinger, was positively droll when he suggested that the choice of a scene that lasted but five seconds was a good reflection on mirror scenes everywhere.

Saturday Night Fever (1977). Mirror, mirror on the wall, who's got the best dance moves of them all? John Travolta does as he stands in front of his mirror in a black Speedo, surrounded by posters of Bruce Lee, Rocky, and Farrah Fawcett. Travolta likes to practice his dance moves every Saturday night while blow drying and brushing his hair. The final touch before he goes

The dartboard in the slow dancing clubhouse features the image of John Travolta (shown here with Karen Lynn Gorney), a major cause in the scarcity of slow dancing scenes in films after the release of *Saturday Night Fever* in 1977.

to the disco is to put on the new shirt he bought on lay-away (and add a few gold chains).

Mr. Skeffington (1944). Okay, before she went sailing in the rain and caught diphtheria and lost her looks and her hair, Bette Davis was so vain she could not pass a mirror without looking into it. And, yes, after Davis got diphtheria, the only time she would look into a mirror was by accident. But mirror scene fans find all this only mildly interesting. What really intrigues them is that by the time Davis had lost her looks and was wearing the wig and the pasty makeup, Claude Rains, who plays the title role, had lost his sight. Even better, since he had never seen her with the wig and the pasty makeup, he remembered her as a beautiful woman. In mirror scene parlance, Rains had become the perfect mirror. Now, every time Davis looks at him and sees the love in his face, she will see herself as he "sees" her—a beautiful woman. Yes, the movie ends here, but many mirror scene fans think this was a big mistake. For them, this is where it really starts to get interesting.

Count Dracula may never walk into a room with a mirror, but Richard Gere will. Mirror scene fans gave the good-looking stud a big hand for the way he used his mirror to choose what to wear from the 40 shirts, 40 ties and 20 sports jackets he owned in *American Gigolo* (1980). However, the club remains adamant about not including mirror scenes that frighten them, such as those from *Poltergeist* (1982) and *Candyman* (1992).

Author's note: Should you ever happen to meet a mirror scene aficionado, it would be wise not ask them why the classic "mirror scene" between Groucho and Harpo Marx in the 1933 film Duck Soup *is not included among the best mirror scenes. Mirror scene fans will then be forced to point out that it was not a mirror being used in that scene—it was only Groucho and Harpo standing on opposite sides of something that looks like a mirror and each imitating what the other does. The reason mirror scene fans hate these moments is because they don't like to be thought of as humorless.*

MODEL AIRPLANE

Empire of the Sun (1987). "Give the kid back his plane!" was the cry heard most at the model airplane scene fan club viewing of this Spielberg gem about a model airplane being separated from a boy who was separated from his parents for the entire length of the Second World War. The plane was the kid's glider, which stays aloft an extraordinarily long time but finally lands in a Japanese army encampment. Causing the outcry is the fact that the Japanese soldiers refuse to give it back to the boy (played wonderfully by Christian Bale). The glider is lost for nearly four years until a young Japanese model airplane fan at the airfield near the boy's prison camp returns it.

Some model airplane scene intellectuals have even suggested that both model plane scenes in this movie employ a storytelling device known as "foreshadowing." It was Spielberg's way of saying that the boy would be lost by his parents when he lost the plane and will be found again when he finds the plane. They may be right. Right after the boy lost his plane, his parents lost him, and right after he found the plane, his parents found him again.

The Fallen Idol (1949). Although paper airplanes are not expressly mentioned in the *Model Airplane Scene Rule Book*, neither are they expressly forbidden. This was the reasoning used to allow the scene featuring the "dart" (as Ralph Richardson calls the paper airplane Bobby Henrey made) to be considered in this category. The scene won its award not because the plane was constructed from paper on which a vital message from Ralph Richardson's mistress was written (like great cigar scenes, great model airplane scenes need have nothing to do with plot), but because, considering the paper airplane was made by a ten-year-old, it flew remarkably well for an indoor flight.

The Flight of the Phoenix (1966). Any model airplane scene lover who ever wanted to fly in his or her model airplane can see his or her fantasy come true in this World War II film starring Jimmy Stewart and Hardy Kruger. But in order to get seven grown men into a model plane, the story must first make sense. This it does. That's because the only way for them to get out of the desert before they die of thirst is to build a plane and the only one who knows how to build a plane is Hardy Kruger. The problem is that the only planes Kruger has ever built were model airplanes. For the record, model airplane scene fans still don't understand why the men lose faith in Kruger when they find this out. Didn't Kruger explain to them that a real airplane is just a model airplane, only bigger? He was right. Kruger builds the biggest model airplane in film history, the men lie down on the wings, and Jimmy Stewart gives them all a wild model airplane ride to safety.

Easy Money (1983). Model airplane scenes are rare to begin with but ones that include the building of a Messerschmitt occur even more infrequently. Practically unique is one in which the actor building the Messerschmitt is Rodney Dangerfield. But it does exist and model airplane scene fans feel it is a classic. The path to Dangerfield's construction of a model airplane isn't hard to follow. To inherit $10 million, he must stop gambling, drinking and womanizing. But it isn't easy, so his wife tells him to get a hobby. The hobby he chooses is model airplanes, very gratifying to model airplane scene fans but hard on Dangerfield. For one thing, he has to build the Messerschmitt in the house, which means he has to listen to his daughter practice the violin. For another, he'd rather be at the racetrack.

When his friend suggests taking a look at the department store he is going to inherit, he jumps at the chance to leave the house. But not before delivering one of the greatest model airplane scene lines in film history. As he passes his wife, he remarks, "There's a Messerschmitt in the kitchen. Clean it up, will ya?"

MOVIE THEATER

The existence of a movie theater scene fan club unknown to the members of the D.O.A. couldn't have created more of a stir among movie fans than if a paleoanthropologist had spotted a new species of Neanderthal buying movie tickets to see *One Million B.C.* There are a number of explanations as to why the movie theater scene fan club had not been discovered before but the most accepted reason is that the clubhouse is located in Brooklyn. A sign that the club is also wealthy is the movie marquee they have built outside their brownstone and the ushers they have hired to direct any stray visitor into their 550-seat-auditorium. The number of seats is about equal to the number of its members, making this group the fan club with the largest membership in the D.O.A. The film most frequently advertised on the club's marquee is *Father of the Bride* (1950), which, according to club members, is the last movie shown at the Royal Theater in *The Last Picture Show* (1971). The real Royal Theater is located in Anarene, the West Texas town where the club's favorite movie theater scenes are set.

The Last Picture Show (1971). This Peter Bogdanovich coming-of-age gem tops the list, not so much because of its movie theater scenes, or the fact that in Anarene, Texas, it only costs a quarter to see a movie, but because for the first time in movie history the closing of a movie house is used to symbolize the death of a small town.

Brief Encounter (1945). "Are you by any chance going to the pictures this afternoon?" This Trevor Howard line to Celia Johnson is so thrilling that many of the club's members have begun to use it to pick up women in coffee shops across the United States. When the film's director, David Lean, shows Howard and Johnson in the theater laughing at the screen at the same time we know these two actors are movie nut soulmates who are going to fall in love. They do fall in love, but the romance is never consummated. Remember, this *is* a British movie. Movie theater scene fans in the United States don't seem to care about this. What they do care about, though, is that no print of the film they have seen so far shows what movie the two lovers are enjoying so much.

Gremlins (1984). Gremlins are a great movie audience, and that's what fans of movie scenes set in movie theaters love to watch. What they don't love to watch is when theaters get blown up, even when they are filled with nasty, cartoon-loving gremlins. This comic-horror film has some other nasty scenes as well, particularly the scene in which a gremlin gets fried in a microwave. But movie theater scene fans are not microwave scene fans. Nor have they even arrived when this happens because the microwave scene is in the middle of the film and the movie theater scene is at the end.

Hannah and Her Sisters (1986). Movie nuts who don't think movie theater scenes have any real value should consider that the movie theater scene in this film may have saved Woody Allen's life. He walked into that Westside movie house suicidal and depressed. He didn't even know what film was playing; he just needed a place to go to clear his head. The movie happens to be *Duck Soup* and the scene we see Allen watching is where the entire cast of the movie is singing "Hail Freedonia." and the Marx Brothers are playing the xylophone on the steel helmets of the soldiers. That's when Allen realizes that if movies like this can be made, it is dumb to think of killing himself. So thanks to the Marx Brothers, Allen decides to stop ruining his life and enjoy it while it lasts. And that may account for his being able to write the most wonderful last line in film history. It happens during Thanksgiving. Allen is hugging Dianne Wiest and she tells him, "I'm pregnant."

Cinema Paradiso (1988). The movie theater scene fan club allowed Arnold Zellermeyer to announce its award for this beautiful film because he liked it so much he named his newsletter after it. The movie stars Philippe Noiret as the projectionist of the one theater in a town in Sicily. Zellermeyer chose two key scenes that are wonderfully connected. The first is of the private screening of a film that the local priest must watch before it is shown to the public. When the priest sees a kissing scene, he rings a bell. Noiret must then stop the film and snip the offending scene out, much to the delight of the little boy he has befriended and whom he allows into his projection room to teach him the business. Later in the film, after Noiret has died, the boy, now a famous film director, goes to his funeral. In the final scene he is given a package that Noiret has left for him. Inside is a reel of all the kissing scenes Noiret had been forced to cut from all the movies. Noiret had spliced them together and left them to the director, who plays them for himself at the film's end.

The Blob (1958). If you happen to be walking past the Colonial Theater in Chester Springs, Pennsylvania, on a day it's playing *Daughter of Horror* (1955), don't go in. Not because it's a lousy flick, but because shortly after you get inside a blood red gelatinous mass will ooze out of the screen and try to swallow you up. Though the movie theater fan club all agreed that the 1988 remake had scarier special effects, they liked the Steve McQueen original a lot more. The trailer isn't bad either: *It crawls! It creeps! It eats you alive!*

The Tingler (1959). Every movie theater scene nut knows what a Tingler is. It's a creature that feeds on fear and lurks in the human body. The Tingler lives in your spine and looks a lot like a centipede. One more thing: it can kill you unless you scream when you are frightened. The scene movie theater fans love the most is when a Tingler escapes on screen during the autopsy of a mute. Because she was unable to scream all her life, the Tingler that escapes from her spine is very large. But Vincent Price saves the day when he turns to the movie audience and warns them, "Scream! Scream for your lives!"

At the reception following the awards ceremony, Zellermeyer told a story that explained why he prefers going to movie theaters by himself. For years his mother had been trying to get his father to go to a movie with her. Finally, he agrees to take her downtown to a first run showing of *Les Girls* (1957). The ride on the A train goes smoothly and they are on time for the three o'clock show. Then, about an hour into the film, just as Gene Kelly is about to kiss

Mitzi Gaynor, Zellermeyer's father turns to his mother and says, "We change at 59th street, right?"

MUSEUM

Night of the Generals (1967). The focus for museum nuts in this thriller set during World War II is not the war but a scene shot in a Paris museum. In the scene, Tom Courtenay, an army corporal, is showing Peter O'Toole through the museum when O'Toole, a German general who murders prostitutes, stops at a self-portrait of Vincent Van Gogh. He is fascinated and stands transfixed. After a closeup of Van Gogh's eyes and a quick cut to O'Toole's eyes, we see that what the general is fascinated by is Van Gogh's madness. Courtenay explains to O'Toole that the self-portrait, known as *Van Gogh in Flames*, was done in the asylum where Van Gogh spent the last three years of his life. O'Toole continues to stare until he nearly faints. Museum scene nuts love scenes in which visitors are affected by the paintings in this way.

The Hot Rock (1972). Visitors to museums don't always go there to stare at paintings. The Dortmunder gang goes there to steal a diamond. The plan is perfect and they get the diamond, but only in a sense — Paul Sand has to swallow it before he is caught. So the gang had to steal it again, this time from a police station. This is of no interest whatsoever to museum scene fans, who stop watching when the museum scene is over. Members have since made an occasional pilgrimage to the Brooklyn Museum after learning that this was where the diamond was stolen from.

The Thomas Crown Affair (1999). To apologize for remaking the Steve McQueen version of this film, Pierce Brosnan pulls a neat little museum trick when he returns the painting he stole. The police are waiting for him. He carries a briefcase and wears a bowler hat. But just as the police lieutenant gives orders to stick with the guy in the bowler hat, the museum is teeming with men in bowler hats. The slick method Brosnan uses to return the stolen painting was inspired by Magritte's famous painting, *The Son of Man*. Museum scene aficionados love the scene when the sprinkler system washes a layer of paint off the painting Brosnan was supposed to have stolen, revealing it was right there in the museum all along.

Topkapi (1964). The heist of an emerald-encrusted dagger at the Topkapi museum in Istanbul makes for a pretty neat museum scene. The dagger is stolen by an acrobatic mute who is suspended from the ceiling to defeat the floor-mounted alarm system. All goes well if you don't count the bird that gets trapped in the museum after the thieves depart, setting off the alarm. The robbery scene is taut and museum fans eat it up because it lasts for a good chunk of the film. The bird is a nice touch because it gives the police inspector the chance, when asked by the thieves about how he knew why they came to Turkey, to say, "A little bird told me." Peter Ustinov, who played one of the thieves, won an Oscar for Best Actor in a Supporting Role even though his role was supposed to go to Peter Sellers.

Night at the Museum (2006). Museum scene fans expected to find some really great museum scenes in a film with the word *museum* in its title. They didn't. Ditto for the 2009 sequel.

The members of the museum scene fan club were devastated to learn that in the movie *Hannibal* (2001), the curator whom Anthony Hopkins eats in order to get his job was the curator of a library, not a museum. To cheer themselves up, they frequently go to the nearest museum, look for a pretty girl staring at a painting and ask her what she's doing Saturday night. If she says, "I'm committing suicide," they respond, "What are you doing Friday night?" Which is just what Woody Allen said when visiting a museum to pick up women in *Play It Again Sam* (1972).

By way of apology, the club membership offered their prized recipe for Hannibal Lector's Three-Layer Onion Casserole. It is one of the dishes Anthony Hopkins ate to keep his appetite in remission after he ate the curator of the library in Florence. It's not for the squeamish.

HANNIBAL LECTOR'S THREE-LAYER ONION CASSEROLE

INGREDIENTS

Three white onions
Three yellow onions
A generous portion of Stilton, well-veined
A healthy chunk of Romano cheese
A cup of Boursin Fine Herb
Butter
½ cup dry white wine

Brush casserole dish with butter. With a very sharp knife, thinly slice two of the yellow onions and layer them over the bottom. Cover with slices of the well-veined Stilton. Thinly slice two of the white onions and layer over the slices of Stilton. Cover with slices of Romano. Slice the remaining onions and layer them over the Romano. Crumble the Boursin over the top and cover with the wine. Put casserole in the oven at 350 degrees for one hour. Serve as a side dish with a nice chianti.

NAME MISPRONUNCIATION

The Third Man (1950). In this scene about a man interrupted from carving roast beef to get his name mispronounced, Joseph Cotten mispronounces Doctor Winkle's name with such innocence that the audience never knows whether he does it on purpose or not. When Winkle is called out from the dining room, Cotten's words ("Dr. Winkle?") and Dr. Winkle's controlled response ("*Vin* ... kle") sends a shiver up the spines of name mispronunciation fans across the country. During the scene, which lasts but a moment, Cotten keeps calling Winkle "Winkle," and Winkle keeps correcting him with "*Vin* ... kle!" The scene is so charged that it becomes difficult for the audience to remember why Cotten had gone there in the first place. Cotten also has a few nice throwaway name mispronunciations. In the early part of the film he keeps calling Trevor Howard "Callahan." In a fit of pique, Howard finally corrects him: "It's Callaway! I'm English. Not Irish!"

Touch of Evil (1958). Given the chance, few actors could ever pronounce the name "Vargas" the way Akim Tamiroff does. In the scene where he is upset at the young punk for throwing acid at Charlton Heston, he grabs the punk by the lapel, shouting, "Who tol' you to throw acid at Whargus!" Yes, Tamiroff has trouble with his V's in a number of films, but coming up with "Whargus" (while wearing an ill-fitting wig that keeps falling off, no less) so enraptured name mispronunciation fans that they voted the film into the award category.

Rain Man (1988). Name mispronunciation fans are particularly fond of this movie starring Dustin Hoffman and Tom Cruise because of its delayed fuse. It isn't until the film is halfway over that we discover that when Cruise was saying "Rain Man" as a two-year-old, he was trying to say "Raymond." Particularly appreciated is the fact that Hoffman knew this all the time but didn't let on.

Gentleman's Agreement (1947). Only Gregory Peck has the stature to pull off the ultimate name mispronunciation in film history—mispronouncing your mother's name — and get away with it. Throughout the entire length of this Elia Kazan Oscar winner, Peck calls his mother (Ann Revere) "Maw." Not once does he call her "Ma," or "Mom," or even "Mother." The fact that Revere never once corrects him is proof of the unselfishness of a mother's love. It also won her roles as the mother of many other Hollywood film stars, including Elizabeth Taylor (*National Velvet*), John Garfield (*Body and Soul*) and Montgomery Cliff (*A Place in the Sun*).

Brazil (1985). The only known instance of computer name mispronunciation takes place in this Terry Gilliam film in which a computer that meant to say "Tuttle" says "Buttle." Apparently, computer name mispronunciation in films is quite serious. Buttle winds up dead, while Tuttle sticks around for the entire film fixing things. Some name mispronunciation buffs think this was because Tuttle was played by Robert De Niro.

Suspicion (1941). After searching through the *Name Mispronunciation Scene Rule Book* in a frantic effort to allow the scenes in which Cary Grant refers to Joan Fontaine as "Monkey Face" to receive a name mispronunciation award, the attempt was abandoned. Though the rules give a lot of leeway regarding what is considered a name mispronunciation, there was no getting around Rule 6. Rule 6 states, "Except in the case of where a 'V' is pronounced as a 'W' [as in *Touch of Evil* and *The Third Man*], a name mispronunciation must begin with the same letter as the person's name to be considered as such." Since the character played by Joan Fontaine is named "Lena," and "Monkey Face" clearly begins with an "M" and not an "L," it could not legally be considered a name mispronunciation and remains what it clearly was intended to be: a cruel term of endearment. Many name mispronunciation psychologists feel the choice of such an unkind nickname for Miss Fontaine was Hitchcock's way of getting her to remain so stiff and self-conscious throughout the film.

NECK BRACE

Grand Illusion (1938). The story is well known in neck brace circles, and it is true. Erich von Stroheim's neck brace was not a result of a World War I injury. The idea was his own. Von Stroheim just appeared on the set one day wearing one. His neck brace diary reveals that he was searching for a way to make the prison camp commandant more interesting and decided that a neck brace was the way to go. It was an inspired idea, for the vintage classic truly comes alive in every scene in which von Stroheim appears.

Best moment: When von Stroheim has to shoot Pierre Fresnay, the French nobleman who had been his prisoner and friend. No doubt von Stroheim was aiming for the leg, as he claims, and a pistol shot at 150 feet is certainly a difficult shot, as the mortally wounded Fresnay says. But, in private, von Stroheim always indicated that if he had not been wearing the damned neck brace, he would have made the shot.

Five Easy Pieces (1970). Perhaps it was a desire to prove that people who wear neck braces can lead active lives that led Ralph Waite to play that vicious game of ping-pong with Jack Nicholson. Was Nicholson too hard on Waite when he beat him 21 to 2? Neck brace scene fans are divided on this question. Those who say Nicholson was too hard on his injured brother (Waite) don't buy the argument that if he had gone easier it would have been a form of condescension.

Neck brace medical experts point out that a score of 21 to 2 is not that unusual when someone with a neck injury plays ping-pong with someone whose neck is not injured. Neck brace psychologists in this group add that the game was also a clever and visual way to show how Nicholson felt about his brother. All agree that it is a superb neck brace scene, probably the only one extant in which an actor wearing one plays ping-pong. Favorite line: Waite, wearing his neck brace, says to Nicholson, "I'm not sure you know of my accident."

Funny Farm (1988). What finally won the neck brace scene fan club over in this loony but likeable Chevy Chase film was the fact that it contains one of the funniest neck brace lines in recent memory. A lawyer, wearing a neck brace that tilts his head up, says to the lawyer in whose office he is sitting,

"You ought to get this ceiling painted once in a while." Neck brace scene fans, not accustomed to humor from lawyers (especially about neck braces), do not think this very funny throwaway line will be topped for a long time to come.

One Flew Over the Cuckoo's Nest (1975). In an extraordinary session, the neck brace scene fan club voted Nurse Ratched's (Louise Fletcher) neck brace scene a special award. Though Fletcher doesn't quite hold a candle to Ralph Waite, it was her ability to pretend not to talk above a whisper after being strangled by Jack Nicholson that made the award unanimous. The inclusion of this scene also allowed Nicholson to brag that he is the only actor in Hollywood directly responsible for two films being given this award.

OPERA

Had it not been for the framed photograph of Fortunio Bonanova at a stoop sale in front of the opera scene clubhouse, an investigative reporter from *Cinema Paradiso* would never have sniffed out the opera connection this Spanish baritone has with these three fine films.

Five Graves to Cairo (1943). Forget the supply dumps that Field Marshal Rommel needs to attack Cairo. Fortunio Bonanova, as the Italian General Sebastiano, is only interested in opera. Feeling sorry for him because Rommel keeps banging on the wall while he sings, the screenwriters rewarded Bonanova with the award for the best opera line in film history. He asks Ann Baxter, "How can you expect a nation that belches to understand a nation that loves to sing?"

Citizen Kane (1941). Though Bonanova had nothing to do with solving the riddle of "Rosebud," he had a lot to do with Dorothy Comingore's debut in the fictional opera *Salammbo*. He was her singing coach and practically had a nervous breakdown trying to get Comingore to hit the right notes. He gave it all he had but it wasn't enough. To let opera scene lovers in on how bad Comingore was, there's a wonderful scene during the performance where the camera starts with a shot of her singing an aria, then moves up and up until we see two stagehands on a scaffold. One stagehand turns to the other and, as we hear Comingore singing, squeezes his nose with the fingers of his hand.

Author's note: Welles, who wrote and directed this film, must have been an opera lover. Rather than spoil a classic opera, Salammbo, the opera Comingore is performing in, is not a real opera and the aria she sings was made up for the film.

Going My Way (1944). Fortunio Bonanova, who plays the conductor of the orchestra in this film, only plays a small role in this Best Picture winner, but he was present in the key scene in which Rise Stevens discovers that the Chuck she always had a crush on (Bing Crosby) is now Father Chuck.

There are also some pretty good opera scenes without Fortunio Bonanova. Those worth noting appear below.

Moonstruck (1987). Cher never looked more beautiful and Puccini never sounded better. The good thing is that when Nicolas Cage, the bad baker brother of Danny Aiello, takes Cher to see *La Boheme*, they fall in love. The bad thing is that during intermission she spots her father (Vincent Gardenia) with another woman.

Apocalypse Now (1979). The Vietnam war is not the best setting for opera. The Metropolitan Opera House would have been a better venue for a performance of *Die Walkurie*. But director Francis Ford Coppola makes it work by substituting helicopter gunships with loudspeakers and napalm for the Valkyrie and a Vietnamese village by the beach for the stage. There's only one drawback: you have to like Wagner.

ORCHESTRA

The Red Shoes (1948). Though Moira Shearer is indeed lovely in her movie debut, it is Marius Goring who holds the main interest of orchestra scene fans. Goring, a young composer, is first spotted in the balcony while watching his music teacher conduct a score for a ballet supposedly written by the teacher. He quickly discovers that it is his own music, which his music teacher has stolen it from him. When we next see Goring, he is the orchestra coach of Anton Walbrook's ballet company. Goring has called an extra rehearsal because he doesn't like the way his piece is being played. Orchestra scene fans feel it was worth paying the orchestra overtime since it resulted in one of the greatest orchestra scene lines in movie history.

When Goring asks one of the musicians, "Do you have a B-flat there?" and the musician answers, "No," Goring responds "Ah, that makes all the difference, doesn't it?"

This scene is also important because it results in Walbrook commissioning Goring to write a new score for the ballet *The Red Shoes*. This leads up to a moment that orchestra scene fans hold very dear—Goring, at the podium, ready to conduct his music, deliberately closing the scorebook and lifting his baton. He is going to conduct his piece without looking at the music!

There are many diehard orchestra scene fans who have privately admitted to having never seen Moira Shearer dance in *The Red Shoes*, because the camera never goes back to Goring at the podium and they feel no reason to stick around any longer.

100 Men and a Girl (1937). Probably the only orchestra ever to play in a lobby is the one Adolphe Menjou gets together made up of unemployed musicians. Menjou's daughter, played by Deanna Durbin, tries to get Leopold Stokowski to conduct. It's the only way they can get a job on radio. (Remember, this was 1937.)

Durbin leads the great conductor into this huge lobby. Suddenly, we hear music. Musicians begin to appear on the balcony and from every corner of the place. They are playing their hearts out. The music is so arousing, so seductive, that Stokowski can't resist. He begins to conduct. There he is, standing in the middle of a lobby, looking up to the balcony for the horns, into a corner for the strings, as he conducts his heart away. It is such a musically satisfying and witty scene that it wins over the hearts of orchestra scene fans everywhere.

The Competition (1980). When Amy Irving's piano goes out of tune while she is "piano-faking" the Mozart, it is a tough break for Mozart fans but a lucky one for Prokofiev lovers. Lucky, too, are orchestra scene fans with a sense of humor. When Sam Wanamaker complains that he might not be in the mood to play the Prokofiev, Lee Remick, Irving's piano teacher, delivers one of the funniest orchestra lines that orchestra scene fans can remember hearing. She storms up to Wanamaker and tells him, "It costs extra to carve 'schmuck' on a tombstone. But you would definitely be worth the expense!" Wanamaker has the grace to laugh, Irving gets a chance to play the Prokofiev, and Remick endears herself to orchestra scene fans for all time.

The Man Who Knew Too Much (1956). Alfred Hitchcock is no friend of orchestra scene fans. He promises us a thrilling orchestra scene in the opening credits and then makes us wait until the movie is practically over before delivering. Happily, orchestra scene fans who do wait are rewarded with a pretty good one. By the time this scene rolls around, they know that when the orchestra gets to the part when the cymbals crash, the prime minister of a foreign country will be assassinated. They also know that Doris Day's son is in the hands of the assassins. Hitchcock, mischievous as ever, makes Day choose between saving her son and listening to an awful piece of music called "Storm Cloud Sonata." She chooses the music, leaving it up to Jimmy Stewart to stop the assassin.

Here, Hitchcock delivers on his promise and gives us the sequence of orchestra scenes that orchestra fans have been waiting for: the pan shot of the orchestra, including a chorus that must number over five hundred women; the cymbals, each resting on its own chair; the assassin, hiding behind a curtain; the prime minister in his box (he actually seems to be enjoying the music); Day, looking frantically from the assassin's box to the prime minister's box; Stewart, rushing madly around Albert Hall while trying to find the assassin's box; the assassin's assistant following the score; the cymbalist picking up the cymbals and getting ready; the assassin's gun, sticking out from behind the curtain; the cymbals finally clashing; Day finally screaming; the gun finally firing; the prime minister finally getting shot (in the arm); Stewart finally wrestling with the assassin; and the assassin finally falling from the balcony.

It should be mentioned (finally) that Hitchcock's secret orchestra scene diary reveals that the reason he chose such awful music was that he knew a decent piece would have been too distracting. What the diary does not explain is why he needed a five-hundred-woman chorus or how the prime minister could possibly enjoy such music.

Named on the first-string team of actors who know their way around a good violin concerto were John Garfield, for choosing his violin over Joan Crawford in *Humoresque* (1946); Vittorio Gassman, for choosing his violin over Elizabeth Taylor in *Rhapsody* (1954); and Stewart Granger, for his masterful portrayal of Niccoltò Paganini in *The Magic Bow* (1947). This last movie in one whose title few orchestra scene fans can remember. What they do remember, however, is the scene in which Granger is playing one of Paganini's violin concertos during a concert in Vienna at a time when Napoleon's troops are about to capture the city. During his performance the concert hall doors swing open, troops surround the audience, and a French general marches down the aisle. But Granger's fiddling so charms the general that he allows the concert to continue and marches back up the aisle in step to Paganini's music and Granger's violin.

PANHANDLING

The Treasure of the Sierra Madre (1948). Most panhandling scene fans consider Humphrey Bogart's panhandling performance in this film to be one of the most satisfying in panhandling movie history. Not once, but three times does Bogart hit on John Huston in the streets of Tampico. His line is always the same: "Could you stake a fellow American to a meal?" It's only after the third time that

Huston gets pissed off. First, he tells Bogart that such impudence never came his way. Then, after he hands Bogart a peso, and another for good measure, Huston tells Bogart that from now on he will have to make his way through life without his assistance. In the main hall of the panhandling movie scene clubhouse there is a large photograph of Bogart paying for the bad haircut he got with one of the pesos Huston gave him. There is also a framed reproduction of Bogart's winning lottery ticket, the one that changed him from a panhandler to a gold prospector and eventually got him killed by Alfonso Bedoya, better known as "Gold Hat."

Unable to come up with a panhandling scene matching the brilliance and importance of this one, panhandling scene fans gave up their cherished recipe for the meal Dobbs, Howard and Curtin were eating the night Bruce Bennett showed up at their campsite, ten hours before he was killed by a Mexican bandit's bullet. This is how Howard made it:

BEANS HOWARD
Two pounds of chopped sirloin
Two large white onions
Two cans of Heinz vegetarian beans
Butter or oil

3 or 4 tomatoes
Mayonnaise
Toast
Dijon mustard

Slowly sauté the onions in plenty of butter (or oil, in Howard's case) until they are pearl grey. Add the chopped meat and stir until brown. Pour two cans of vegetarian beans over the onions and meat and continue to stir until the beans are hot. Serve with toast, sliced tomatoes, mayonnaise and mustard. Tastes best when eaten outdoors from a tin plate while scraping the fork against the plate as you speak these words between mouthfuls: "Better have some beans, boys." Scrape, scrape. "You sure you won't have some beans?" Scrape, scrape scrape.

Serves 3 with enough left over for an unexpected guest.

PARKING METER

Playtime (1967). Only the incomparable Jacques Tati could find joy in something that was designed to make people so nervous. Tati saves his memorable parking meter moment for the final scene of this film. To set it up, he first gives us a shot of a Parisian traffic circle crowded with cars, trucks and tour buses going slowly round and round and round to the music of a carousel. Suddenly, the traffic and music stop. Into camera range walks Tati, who instantly sizes up the situation and does something that underscores his unique parking meter sensibility: he puts a coin in a parking meter. The moment he does this, the traffic and carousel music start up again. Tati then walks off as if putting a coin in a parking meter to start up traffic again is the most natural occurrence in the world. This is not only a brilliant and original use of a parking meter, but also a genuinely funny and fresh scene. Many parking meter fans feel that if Tati is to be remembered for just one screen moment, this should be it.

Cool Hand Luke (1967). One reason there have been so few parking meter scenes to choose from may be due to this Warner Bros. release. When Paul Newman saws off the tops of those parking meters, he nearly exterminates the parking meter population in Hollywood. Few parking meter scene devotees can watch this scene without mixed feelings. They appreciate the scene's unique qualities, but at the same time understand that it had two grave consequences: It resulted in Newman being sent to the prison where he was shot by the guard who always wore sunglasses, and Newman's wanton destruction of those parking meters resulted in the filming of only two parking meter scenes since.

Bananas (1971). A direct result of the parking meter shortage caused by Paul Newman in *Cool Hand Luke* four years earlier is the parking meter scene in this Woody Allen release, which had to be shot without a parking meter. In Allen's now famous dream sequence, four monks carrying a large wooden cross upon which Woody Allen is tied start backing into a parking space. Another four monks carrying a large wooden cross to which someone else is tied start to park their cross in the same parking space and a fistfight breaks out.

Allen's secret notes for the film reveal that he intended to have the winning monks park the cross and deposit a coin in a parking meter. But no meter could be found in Hollywood and it was written out of the scene. It might be interesting to note here that until Allen's notes for the dream sequence were found, this scene was thought to be an alternate-side-of-the-street parking scene.

PICKPOCKET

Casablanca (1942). Better known for the greatest last line in film history (when Humphrey Bogart turns to Claude Rains and says, "Louie, I think this is the beginning of a beautiful friendship"), this film also has a nice little pickpocket scene right at the beginning. Many pickpocket scene movie nuts feel that it's the pickpocket himself who sets up the colorful and desperate atmosphere of Casablanca. First he warns the rich American couple to watch out for pickpockets. Then he leaves.

The waiter comes with the check. The rich old guy goes for his wallet. It's no longer there. But the poor sap still doesn't get it and he turns to his wife to say, "I must have left my wallet in the hotel." But we all know he didn't. The pickpocket comes back for a funny little encore when he accidentally bumps into S.Z. Sakall at Rick's American Bar. After the bump, Sakall, who knows all about this guy, checks his pockets to make sure everything is there.

The Hunchback of Notre Dame (1939). Pickpocket blundering has its upside — you get to marry Maureen O'Hara. The only scene pickpocket fans watch in this film is when Thomas Mitchell, chief of the beggars, calls to bring in "The Bell Boy." Mitchell stuffs a purse in its pocket and orders Edmond O'Brien to pick the purse without any of the bells jangling or he will be hanged. O'Brien fails. He is about to be hanged when someone reminds Mitchell about the rule that any man about to be hanged will be spared if any of the women will marry him. Maureen O'Hara pushes her way through the crowd and says, "I'll take him," and O'Brien is allowed to live ... until he is poisoned in *D.O.A.*

The Sting (1973). It's rare that a pickpocket scene affects a movie's plot as much as it does in this film. When Eileen Brennan bumps into Robert Shaw in the corridor of the 20th Century Limited train to Chicago and "lifts" Shaw's wallet, Paul Newman has enough money to play in the poker game run by Shaw. Shaw loses and when he reaches for his wallet to pay up, his money's not there. This gives Newman a chance to berate him and Redford, as part of the sting, a chance to ingratiate himself with Shaw to start the sting operation rolling.

Executive Suite (1954). A short piece on page 6 of *Cinema Paradiso* confirmed that the heart attack fan club lost its court battle with pickpocket movie nuts to list this film within its category. The D.O.A. ruled that because the actor who had the heart attack was never seen on screen, the heart attack was ruled null and void. Pickpocket fans had little time to cheer because the D.O.A. later ruled that the pocket of Avery Bullard (the name of the character played by the actor whose face never appears on screen) had not been picked. Bullard was holding his wallet in his hand when he collapsed and the wallet fell to the ground and was then picked up by a dishonest passerby.

The Man Who Would Be King (1975). If you're going to pick someone's pocket, make sure he isn't a Freemason. When Michael Caine lifts the watch from Christopher Plummer and notices the symbol of Freemasonry on the watch chain, being a brother mason, he has to give it back. That good deed leads to the death of Sean Connery and causes Caine to lose everything, including his mind. Connery must have forgiven him because two years later the two appeared in *A Bridge Too Far*.

PLAGIARISM

The Red Shoes (1948). The best ballet movie ever made also contains a neat little plagiarism scene. After Marius Goring's music professor steals his music and passes it off as his own, the plagiarism scene fan club never ceases to be shocked when Anton Walbrook advises Goring to do nothing about it. "The professor may have the name, but you have the genius." Walbrook goes on to tell Goring to imagine how bad the professor must feel knowing he had to steal Goring's music to stay on top. Goring takes Walbrook's advice, gets to fall in love with Moira Shearer and goes on to write the score for the ballet *The Red Shoes.*

You Will Meet a Tall Dark Stranger (2010). Never plagiarize from someone who gives you a manuscript to read unless you're absolutely sure he's dead. Josh Brolin, a washed-up writer, does so in this Woody Allen movie and then learns at the end of the film that the guy whose book he stole has just woken up from his coma. This is why fans of actors who play writers who have been plagiarized are getting people to send Josh Brolin this e-mail: *So what happened to the manuscript I asked you to read?*

The Front (1976). Passing off the work of a blacklisted scriptwriter as your own in exchange for ten percent so you can help him earn a living isn't the classic definition of plagiarism. Members of the plagiarism scene fan club prefer to call it anti–McCarthyism. Still, Woody Allen, a cashier in a diner, likes the attention he gets as a writer, even though he hardly reads the scripts he turns in. The only drawback to Allen's plagiarism is when he goes to a singles weekend. Once he tells the women he meets that he's a writer, they walk away. But Allen is no dummy. He tells the next woman he meets that he is a pediatric dentist with a thriving practice. Pretty soon he is surrounded by women who want to meet him.

Good Will Hunting (1997). The scene where Matt Damon puts down a graduate student in a bar who is making fun of Ben Affleck by spouting lines from a book on economics shows that verbal plagiarism can also make a good movie scene. Damon cuts the grad student down to size by asking him if he has any thoughts of his own on the subject or is he just gonna plagiarize the whole book? Library scene fans particularly like it when Damon tells the grad student that he just dropped a hundred and fifty grand on an education that he could have picked up for a dollar fifty in late charges at the public library.

POISON

Arsenic and Old Lace (1944). Elderberry wine is the drink of choice in the poison scene fan club and Josephine Hull and Jean Adair know how to serve it. For a gallon of elderberry wine, you take one teaspoon full of arsenic, then add half a teaspoon of strychnine, and then just a pinch of cyanide. The victims are all lonely old men who are then buried in the cellar. It helps to have a crazy nephew who thinks he is Teddy Roosevelt. All the ladies have to do is tell their nephew the poisoned old men were yellow fever victims. Teddy's bugle and his cry of "charge" are nice touches. So is the supporting cast that includes Raymond Massey as a psychopathic nephew and his sidekick Dr. Einstein (Peter Lorre). Best poison line in the film is when Josephine Hull tells Cary Grant, "One of our gentlemen found time to say, 'How delicious.'" It is rumored that after making the film Grant laid off wine for 18 months.

Godfather III (1990). Talia Shire may not rank up there with Josephine Hull as a poisoner but members of the Best Poison Scene Fan Club still rate her pretty high. It may be true that no member of the club has seen the entire *Godfather* trilogy, but it's certain that every one of them saw Don Altobello (Eli Wallach) eat the poisoned cannoli she prepared for him on his birthday. What may have put this scene over the top is that Wallach was seated alone in his box at the opera house when he ate the cannoli.

D.O.A. (1950). What's not to like about a movie that begins with a man walking into a police station to report his own murder? The movie (not the organization for which it is named) was a shoo-in for its award even though Edmond O'Brien sends his drink back because it tastes funny (Rule #7 in the Best Poison Scene Handbook states that the victim should not be able to detect the poison he is drinking or eating). The poison is identified as iridium. It's also referred to as a "luminous toxin" because when the doctor shows

O'Brien the test tube of the liquid he took from O'Brien's body, it glows in the dark.

The Princess Bride (1987). Few actors know their way around a good poison scene like Wallace Shawn. After he switches the goblets and drinks, Shawn boasts to Cary Elwes that though the wisdom of never getting into a land war in Asia is widely known, lesser known is the axiom of never going against a Sicilian when death is on the line. He then drops dead. Fans of Wallace Shawn are grateful that *My Dinner with Andre* (1981) was made before *Princess Bride* so that Shawn could fully enjoy the meal he and Andre Gregory eat during that entire film.

The Court Jester (1955). "The pellet with the poison's in the vessel with the pestle. The chalice from the palace has the brew that is true." This is recited in unison by the members of the poison scene fan club before they vote on the best poison scenes in film history. But before they can vote, the member who looks most like Griselda (Mildred Natwick) rushes in to announce that there's been a change: "The chalice from the palace has been broken. Now the pellet with the poison is in the flagon with the dragon. The vessel with the pestle has the brew that is true!" At this point all the members throw up their hands and head for the nearest bar, where an honorary vassal fills all the vessels with Dewars White Label.

Kind Hearts and Coronets (1949). When the Reverend Lord Henry D'Ascoyne (Alec Guinness) tells Dennis Price that "the port is with you," fans of poison scenes become so excited they find it hard to swallow. When Price puts the poison in Guinness's glass of port, he gets one step closer to becoming the tenth Duke of Chalfont. For poison purists, the only thing that mars this poisoning scene is that Price chops down the D'Ascoyne family tree by other means, including bomb, arrow and gunshot.

It should be noted that the poison that Colonel Klebb (Lotte Lenya) tried to administer to James Bond (Sean Connery) in *From Russia with Love* (1963) was not allowed because the poisoned razor in Colonel Klebb's shoe does not qualify as poison administered in a drink or a dish. The Bear Clan Queen's poisoned fingernail in the underrated *Thirteenth Warrior* (1999) is not listed for the same reason.

PRISON

White Heat (1949). Probably the best of the prison scene genre, and certainly the most carefully choreographed, is that memorable moment when Jimmy Cagney finds out his mother is dead. First, Cagney spots a new prisoner seated about six people away from where he is eating. Then, he whispers to the prisoner next to him to find out from the new prisoner how his mother is doing. The message is passed along (in whispers) until the new prisoner gets it. He then passes back the answer, from inmate to inmate, until the prisoner next to Cagney says in a stage whisper, "She's dead." This is the moment Cagney, who has always been something of a momma's boy, was waiting for. His reaction is known and loved by prison scene fans all over the world. First, Cagney starts to whine; then he bangs his head on the table; and then he climbs on the table and starts to crawl over everybody's lunch. When the guards try to stop him, he punches three of them out until he is finally subdued.

Proof of the high regard in which this scene was held is the D.O.A.'s speedy squashing of a food mushing fan bid to place this scene in their category. A spokesman for the D.O.A. had this to say about the food mushing change-of-venue request: "Calling the Jimmy Cagney lunchroom scene a food mushing scene would be like calling *Treasure of the Sierra Madre* a movie about bad haircuts." An apology was made to all haircut scene fans who took offense at this analogy and the matter was dropped.

Kind Hearts and Coronets (1949). This highly gratifying British film has a neat little prison scene. Dennis Price, who has murdered Guinness eight times so he could inherit the title and name of Gascoyne-Dascoyne, is in prison charged with a murder he did not commit. He spends the time in prison writing in his diary about how he murdered all the Gascoyne-Dascoynes who were ahead of him in line for the title.

When it is finally proved that Price is innocent of the crime of which he has been accused, he walks out of the prison, only to realize he has left his diary in his cell. Though prison scene fans frown on prison scenes that have anything to do with the denouement of a film, Price's elegant prison manners and the final shot of his diary in the cell being read by the prison guards packed enough of a wallop to sway the vote in his favor.

Angels with Dirty Faces (1938). Few prison scene admirers will ever forgive Pat O'Brien for asking James Cagney to pretend to be afraid when they march him off to the electric chair so the Dead End Kids won't think a killer was a hero. Cagney, a veteran of many prison movies, takes it all in good grace. He breaks down on his last walk to the "chair" but never lets on whether he did it because O'Brien asked him to or because he was really afraid. In the end, it was Cagney's effortless prison deportment that gave him a second prison laurel and earned this scene its award.

Take the Money and Run (1969). When Woody Allen vows that he will never serve out his full term, prison scene fans know they are in for a special treat. They are not disappointed. Allen first gives them a prison escape in which the character he plays fashions a gun from a bar of soap and shoe polish. If it hadn't raining, the escape would have been successful. Unfortunately, the guards become suspicious when the gun turns to soap bubbles. Allen's second attempt to leave prison early is less ingenious, but more successful, as it leads to a parole. To get the parole, he volunteers to test a new vaccine. The vaccine has only one side effect: for several hours Allen is turned into a rabbi (a prison first).

These scenes alone are enough to satisfy even the most demanding prison scene enthusiast, but Allen isn't through. He has one great prison scene left. It is the classic escape after he is sent back to prison for a second term. The escape works, but there are problems. When nobody tells him that the break has been called off, Allen finds himself in the prison courtyard being laughed at by his fellow inmates. Allen, remarkably resourceful, has the last laugh — he takes a cab and makes his escape. Prison fans were particularly pleased with "Virgil Starkwell" as Allen's choice of name for the character he played. On a prisoner name authenticity scale of one to ten, it rated a 9.8, with "Al Capone" being the only prisoner name to receive a higher rating.

The sudden lack of a quorum due to parole violations by two members of the prison scene fan club curtailed any further voting. Among the films that were up for an award were the following: *I Want to Live* (1958), starring Susan Hayward; *Brute Force* (1947), starring Hume Cronyn and Burt Lancaster; *Birdman of Alcatraz* (1962), starring Burt Lancaster and Karl Malden; *Calling Northside 777* (1948), starring James Stewart; and *20,000 Years in Sing Sing* (1933), starring Spencer Tracy and Bette Davis. Because this lack of a quorum has happened on more than one occasion, the Prison Scene Fan Club Rules Committee recently decided to accept write-in ballots.

PSYCHIATRIST

Spellbound (1945). Psychiatrist scene movie nuts could have chosen the scene in which Ingrid Bergman helps Gregory Peck remember what he saw in the snow that day but they didn't. Instead, they chose the scene where Bergman's old teacher (Michael Chekov) tells her, "Women make the best psychiatrists. Until they fall in love. Then they make the best patients."

Deconstructing Harry (1997). No one ever accused the psychiatrist scene fan club of having high cultural aspirations. Proof of this is the scene they picked in which Kirstie Alley is cursing out Woody Allen for sleeping with one of her patients. That the scene is shot in the midst of a session with another patient is a stroke of Allen genius. When Alley asks the patient to excuse her for a minute in order to tell Allen, "You fuck! I can't believe it. You fucked my patient!" the club members are at the edge of their couches. Woody's excuse for sleeping with her patient is pretty neat. He explains to Alley that he's home writing all day, so where else is he going to meet women? In the scene's hilarious climax, Kirstie returns to her patient on the couch and shouts a final "Motherfucker!" through the door, causing the poor patient to dissolve into tears.

The Manchurian Candidate (1962). Dr. Yen Lo isn't the kind of doctor who is going to get a lot of referrals through the HMO, but he can be pretty effective nevertheless. Played by the great character actor Khigh Dhiegh in this still-riveting 1962 political thriller, he's the psychiatrist who makes war hero Raymond Shaw (Laurence Harvey) shoot both the girl he loves and her father. So, should you ever find yourself on a date with a member of the psychiatrist scene fan club and he (or she) says, "Why don't we pass the time by playing a little solitaire?" then it might be a good idea to make some excuse to leave.

Good Will Hunting (1997). To the psychiatrist scene fan club, it's not all the good advice Robin Williams gives Matt Damon that put this film on the best psychiatrist scene list. It's when Damon slyly asks psychiatrist George Plimpton if he finds it hard to hide the fact that he's gay.

Analyze This (1999). When psychiatrist Billy Crystal tells Mafia boss Robert De Niro to hit a pillow whenever he gets mad and De Niro pulls out a gun and blasts the pillow to feathers, we know we're in for a pretty good psychiatrist movie scene. The fact that De Niro insists on clandestine meetings to avoid being "whacked by the mob" adds a frisson of pleasure to their scenes together.

What About Bob? (1991). What movie nut can fail to love a psychiatrist (Richard Dreyfuss) who points a rifle at his patient (Bill Murray) because he followed him on his sacred August vacation and won't leave him alone? When Murray asks what he's doing, Dreyfuss tells him it's death therapy, a guaranteed cure. Dreyfuss has an equally good moment earlier in the film. When Murray calls him Leo at the dinner table, Dreyfuss tells him, "You can only call me Leo in my office. In my home, it's Dr. Marvin."

Notes from the voting minutes of the psychiatrist's movie scene fan club revealed that the reason none of the psychiatrist scenes in *Prince of Tides* (1991) made the list was because the members felt that Barbra Streisand's fingernails were too long during her sessions with Nick Nolte.

RESTAURANT

Five Easy Pieces (1970). Maybe it was just to prove he could do it, but Jack Nicholson almost gets the side order of toast he wanted with his omelet. The moment they hear him say to the bitchy waitress, "I'll make it easy for you. You've got bread and a toaster of some kind?" the toes of restaurant scene fans start wiggling. Nicholson then orders a chicken salad sandwich on toast, hold the mayo and the lettuce and tells the waitress to hold the chicken salad ... and stick it between her legs. That's when he gets thrown out. After searching through restaurant scene records, it was determined that no actor got more applause for his bad restaurant manners. The surprise here is that not one member of the club ever asked what kind of restaurant won't give you a side order of toast.

The Godfather (1972). One rule fans of restaurant scenes have learned is to not let their dates go to the men's room while they're having dinner at an Italian restaurant. Sterling Hayden never learned that rule and got shot in the head before he even finished his veal scallopine.

Pretty Woman (1990). Julia Roberts got high marks from the membership. Not only did she know how to play a kind-hearted streetwalker, she also knew how to throw a perfect snail pass to the waiter with her escargot.

My Dinner with Andre (1981). Not many moviegoers know that Andre Gregory once worked with a group of Polish actors in a forest in Poland, but restaurant scene movie nuts know. It's the kind of conversation that the more intellectual restaurant scene fans like to hear. The only downside of this film is that because the entire movie takes place in a restaurant, fans are forced to sit through the entire film. Fortunately, Wallace Shawn and Gregory are brilliant, and so is the meal. A pleasant surprise is the marvelous Jean Lenauer, who plays the old waiter.

When Harry Met Sally (1989). Restaurant scene aficionados admit they don't like it when Meg Ryan orders her corned beef sandwich on white bread with mayonnaise. But they excuse her when she shows Billy Crystal how a woman can fake an orgasm while having lunch with him in Katz's delicatessen. In private, they admit that the best part of that scene comes afterward, when the woman at a nearby table tells the waiter, "I'll have what she's having."

Deception (1946). If you think Jack Nicholson was an expert at getting what he wanted in *Five Easy Pieces*, check out Claude Rains in this movie. He tells the waiter he'd like "a nice brook trout, not too large, from a good stream."

Get Shorty (1995). Restaurant scene enthusiasts are continually amazed at how many actors know how to get just what they want when ordering. In the scene at the Ivy in Beverly Hills, Danny DeVito doesn't even need a menu. He orders an egg-white omelet with shallots. Only he wants the shallots browned slightly with a little olive oil ... and no salt. The best part of the scene is that DeVito leaves before his omelet even arrives.

The Million Pound Note (1954). Gourmands in the restaurant scene fan club love scenes where a starving, penniless seaman walks into a four-star restaurant and orders a five-course meal and then eats everything on every plate set before him. That's what Gregory Peck does in 1904 London. When the bill arrives, club members are at the edges of their seats. In Peck's pocket is a one million pound note given to him by two wealthy men. They have made a bet. One of the men wagered that anyone carrying a one million pound note would never have to cash it. The other said he would have to. Peck gives the million pound note to the waiter, who shows it to the owner. The bug-eyed owner says to give Peck whatever he wants. Club members love what Peck says when he hears this: "In that case, I'll have the same again."

One member pointed out that the scene is a typical example of how banks are only willing to lend money to people who already have money, but his argument didn't get very far.

The Iron Lady (2011). Just before accepting her future husband's proposal of marriage, the young Margaret Thatcher (Alexandra Roach) warns him that she doesn't want to die washing a teacup.

Only when the young Denis Thatcher agrees does she accept his proposal and they proceed to do a lovely waltz around the restaurant to the tune of "Shall We Dance" from *The King and I*. Ironically, marriage proposal aficionados never see the end of the film when Thatcher, now played by the wonderful Meryl Streep, is left alone washing up a teacup in her kitchen — something she had promised Denis she would never do.

Author's note: Yes, the scene takes place in a restaurant. And yes, there is a marriage proposal. But the by-laws of the D.O.A. stipulate that when it is impossible to determine which category a scene should be placed in, it is settled the old-fashioned way — by a coin toss. Cyril Delavanti, the restaurant scene fan club president, called heads and won.

Restaurant scene movie nuts eat it up when food winds up on someone's lap, so Gregory Peck gets a big thumbs up when Lauren Bacall dumps a plate of spaghetti on his lap in *Designing Woman* (1957). Jacques Tati also receives high marks for his ability to keep eating while the swinging door to the seaside hotel dining room makes that creaking noise every time the waiter goes in or out in *Mr. Hulot's Holiday* (1953). Tati is also the only one in the resort who notices that the saltwater taffy is melting off the hook and keeps putting it back before it hits the ground. A brilliantly funny scene in a movie that's filled with brilliantly funny scenes.

RUNNING

The Naked Prey (1966). There's not a lot of dialogue but there is a lot of running, which suits fans of running scenes to a tee. Cornell Wilde is the running prey. He is stripped naked and given a brief head start, then chased by some of the tribesmen. With a combination of luck, cunning, and desperation, he eludes the warriors, killing several; finds food and water; and, after many days, reaches a colonial fort just seconds ahead of his pursuers. The salute he exchanges with the leader of the men chasing him is a nice touch.

The Loneliness of the Long Distance Runner (1962). The scenes of Tom Courtenay, a Borstal prisoner, training for the big race with a prestigious public school are lovely. Just watching Courtenay run through the English countryside gives running scene fans the same emotional and physical release that Courtenay gets. There are lots of shots of trees and sky and a jazzy score by the British heavy metal group Iron Maiden. But the scene that really gets the hearts of running scene fans pumping is when Courtenay, ahead in the race, defiantly stops and lets the other runners pass. The expression on Michael Redgrave's face, who as headmaster thought a win would boost his career, is worth the price of admission alone. Movie fans who aren't running scene nuts might recognize James Fox as the lead runner of the private school in those final scenes. Fox became a fine actor but you would never know it by the way he runs, a sort of self-conscious lope that has to be seen to be believed.

Apocalypto (2006). The Running Scene Rule Book says it's okay to have two running scenes up for consideration in which a runner has to run for his life. Even so, most running scene fans privately agree that Mel Gibson, who directed this film in the jungles of Yucatan, at least owes Cornell Wilde a nice dinner.

Forrest Gump (1994). Fans of running scenes like it most when Forrest Gump explains why he went on that run: "That day, for no particular reason, I decided to go for a little run. So I ran to the end of the road, and when I got there, I thought maybe I'd run to the end of town. And when I got there, I thought maybe I'd just run across Greenbow County. And I figured since I run this far, maybe I'd just run across the great state of Alabama. And that's what I did. I ran clear across Alabama." A good way for movie audiences to tell how far Gump ran is to check out the beard he grew during the run. Gump also drew a nice crowd. They followed him most of the way.

Chariots of Fire (1981). Watch a group of runners on a beach and it's only mildly interesting. Add the stirring *Chariots of Fire* theme music by Albert Vergalis and some wet sand on the runners' faces and you have the ingredients of an unforgettable running scene. And that's only the opening scene of the movie. There are three other running scenes worth mentioning. Ben Cross winning the 100 meter at the 1923 Olympics in France is wonderful, but the scene that gets the hearts of running scene movie nuts racing is set in a hotel room opposite the Olympic stadium. When Cross's running coach, Ian Holm, sees the British flag being raised over the stadium and hears the British anthem being played, he is so overcome with emotion that he punches his fist through his straw hat. Even better is the scene in which Ian Charleston, the Scottish missionary, wins the 400 meter. The camera slows down, the theme music is cued, and Charleston lifts his head in the pure pleasure of running. It's not hard to understand why Charleston says, "If God didn't want me to run, why did he make me so fast?"

Rocky (1976). The Philadelphia Museum of Art may have a lot of nice paintings inside, but it is most famous for the steps that Rocky Balboa races up, raising his arms in triumph at the top. Every year, thousands of tourists create their own *Rocky* moment by running up those same stairs. Members of the running scene fan club must do it at least once a year to keep their membership current.

10 (1979). Fine comic actor Dudley Moore was voted a posthumous lifetime membership in the club for traveling all the way to Mexico to watch Bo Derek in her bikini and corn rows run along the beach. The lifetime membership also included a medal for Moore's uncomplaining bravery in enduring the hot sand until his feet reached the ocean. However, the club also felt that Blake Edward's charge that Hugh Hudson, the director of *Chariots of Fire*, stole the slow-motion running in the sand idea from him was false and defamatory. To avoid a libel suit, the members persuaded Edwards to drop the charge.

Marathon Man (1976). It should be noted that because Dustin Hoffman was running to escape from the dentist, not to save his life, the running scene along the Central Park reservoir was allowed to be entered for purse money only.

SAGGING SHOULDERS

Breaking the Sound Barrier (1947). Many have heard the rumors: Ralph Richardson improvised the scene; the director was afraid to attempt it even though it was in the shooting script; Richardson had done the scene 21 times and was simply tired. Whichever is true, the sagging shoulders scene in this British film stands so far above all others in the category that sagging shoulders scene fans closed the voting after its selection.

The great moment occurs when Denholm Elliot, Richardson's son, crashes his Spitfire while trying to land during his first solo flight. At the moment of impact, Richardson, who had been watching the flight with his back to the camera, allows his shoulders to sag with such expression that the audience knows instantly he really loved his son despite the fact that he was a lousy pilot. They also know that Richardson is sorry for forcing him to take flying lessons even though he knew Elliot hated flying.

To be sure, there are other sagging shoulders scenes that were up for an award. One desperate clique of sagging shoulders scene fans insisted that Marlon Brando's sagging shoulders scene after his defeat in the battle of Waterloo in *Desiree* (1954) be included. Another group was in favor of giving Oscar Humulka's slumping shoulders reaction in *War and Peace* (1956) an award. But the majority of sagging shoulders scene fans held firm. Their argument was hard to refute: a good sagging shoulders scene is not a great sagging shoulders scene.

When informed that they might lose their accreditation with the D.O.A. because of the paucity of their selections (one scene in five years), the members of the sagging shoulders scene fan club agreed to give up something they cherished nearly as much as sagging shoulders scenes—their recipe for the perfect medium-boiled egg. The offer was accepted and this amazingly simple way to make a perfect medium-boiled egg is revealed here for the first time.

THE PERFECT MEDIUM-BOILED EGG

Fill a pot with water. Place two eggs into pot. Light the burner. When the water starts to boil, put a slice of bread into the automatic toaster. When the toast pops up, remove the eggs from the pot and serve.

Author's note: I have tried this recipe many times, and it has not failed me once.

SHADOW

The untimely breakup of the shadow scene fan club, caused by the inability of a single member to name the movie in which Goliath cast his giant shadow over David, unfortunately took place before the members were scheduled to vote on their selections. A chance meeting with the former scribe of the defunct organization enabled me to obtain a copy of his notes, which contain a partial listing of some of the scenes the former members were considering. I was given permission to make them public after promising to make no changes. They are re-created on these pages verbatim.

The Gay Divorcee (1934). Ingenious idea ... paper cutouts on a record player turntable. Lampshade. Spinning round and round, making shadow on wall that looks like two people dancing ... allows Fred Astaire and Ginger Rogers to sneak out while everyone thinks they're up there dancing. Find out name of tune. Is it "Continental" or "Night and Day"? Check if there is a record player fan club. Will there be any trouble with them on this?

Citizen Kane (1941). Check with D.O.A. to see if any other club is considering this movie for award. Did Comingore really think Welles making his finger look like a rooster shadow was funny?

The Magnificent Ambersons (1942). Welles again! This time responsible for putting Joseph Cotten's shadow on door of dead father's room and telling him to walk closer so shadow will loom bigger and bigger.

Infidelity scene fans have all agreed never to invite Bette Davis (right) and Gale Sondergaard to the same party after what happened in *The Letter* (1940).

The Third Man (1950). Check with lawyer on status of restraining order re: balloon vendor shadow. Is it ours or not?

The Letter (1940). Set up screening. Find out if clouds passing over moon obscuring Gale Sondergaard's face count as shadows; if affirmative, put spelling of Sondergaard's name on admissions test to club.

Except for a personal note to check the TV listings for the time that *Shadow of the Thin Man* (circa 1940) comes on, this was the final entry.

SHAVING

Guess Who's Coming to Dinner (1967). Never drink scotch while you're shaving. Spencer Tracy learns this the hard way when he dips his shaving brush into his scotch glass. The shaving scene fan club voted this into the best scene category anyway because Tracy had a good reason for his shaving faux pas — Sidney Poitier was coming to dinner and wanted to marry his daughter.

Mississippi Burning (1988). One of the lessons that the Mississippi deputy sheriff (Brad Dourif) learns in this movie is to not get a shave when

Gene Hackman is the barber, and especially not when Hackman is pissed off that Dourif has beaten up his wife (Frances McDormand). After being nicked a few times on the cheek and neck, Dourif faints and Hackman leaves (but not before spinning Dourif around a few times in the barber chair).

My Darling Clementine (1946). "What kind of town is this anyway?" That's what Henry Fonda asks when he can't get a shave in the Tombstone barbershop because a drunk is shooting up the bar. After a few bullets break the barbershop's window, Fonda gets up, goes into the bar and knocks out the drunk before he gets back in the chair for his shave. Barbershop fans like the fact that Fonda uses that "What kind of town is this anyway?" line in practically every western he acted in.

High Plains Drifter (1973). Clint Eastwood doesn't let anyone interrupt his shave in this supernatural western. When three bad guys try it halfway through his straight-razor shave, he shoots them. Eastwood gets his shave finished but only after the barber stops shaking.

The Great Dictator (1940). Only the great Charlie Chaplin would think of choreographing a straight-razor shaving scene to Brahms's Hungarian Dance #5. Chaplin is marvelous as he applies the shaving cream, shaves, sharpens the razor and towels the customer all in tune with the music. Members agree that it is the looks on the poor customer's face as Chaplin gives him a shave in time to the music that puts this scene over the top. Also very satisfying among club members, who spend an average of $40 a haircut for men and $75 a haircut for women, is the final moment when Chaplin sticks out his hand and says, "10 cents please."

SHOE

The Wizard of Oz (1939). Judy Garland's ruby slippers always catch the attention of shoe scene movie nuts when the shoes are first spotted on the feet of the Wicked Witch of the East. They were the slippers the Wicked Witch was wearing when Dorothy, Toto and the house from Kansas fell on her. Even though moviegoers never see the Wicked Witch of the East alive, the sight of the ruby slippers sticking out from under the house makes this a shoe scene for all ages. The public relations campaign promoting Dorothy's ruby slippers was so successful that the slippers are now displayed at the Smithsonian Institution and have become one of its most asked-about artifacts.

The Devil Wears Prada (2006). In a movie filled with four-inch stiletto heels, shoe scene fans chose to vote for a scene with no stiletto heels and no dialogue. The winner is the look Meryl Streep gives Anne Hathaway when the camera follows Streep's gaze down and we see Hathaway wearing flats. Stanley Tucci's remark when he sees Hathaway came in a close second. He looks at her from head to toe and asks Streep, "Are we doing a 'before and after' piece?"

Best in Show (2000). This movie about a dog show is hilarious for many reasons, not the least of which is the shot of Christopher Guest's shoes. To the delight of shoe scene fans, Guest claims that he was born with two left feet, and when the camera lingers on his feet it proves that he was: Guest is wearing two left shoes.

Cinderella (1950). The ritual hiding of Cinderella's glass slipper is a lot like the ritual hiding of the matzoh during the Passover seder. Until the matzoh is found, the seder can't continue. And until the members of the shoe scene fan club find the hidden glass slipper, they can't watch the scene where the Prince tries the slipper on everyone in his kingdom until he finally slips it onto Cinderella's dainty foot.

Hannah Montana (2009). How good can a movie be when it's based on a Disney TV sitcom? Very good, say shoe scene movie critics. They argue that any film that contains the only shoe fight in film history deserves attention. The scene starts when Hannah (Miley Cyrus) and Tyra Banks both want the same pair of stiletto shoes. During the shoe hissy fit, Hannah, frustrated that she can't reach the other shoe when six-footer Tyra holds it up, winds up throwing the stiletto shoe she has at Banks. It misses her by inches and gets stuck in the wall, heel first. Lousy movie, yes. But a great shoe fight.

Strangers on a Train (1951). The way has been cleared for this suspenseful Hitchcock masterpiece of how two completely different pairs of shoes can meet on a train and exchange murders to be placed in the shoe scene category where it belongs. Mistakenly labeled as a train scene for nearly two decades, it has finally been recognized for what it is — one of the best shoe scenes in film history. The arguments for the change in category were beyond repute. First, the movie opens with the camera focused on two pairs of shoes, not on the train station. Second, the shoes meet on the train and the psychotic black-and-white spectator shoes suggest to the normal pair of shoes that they swap murders.

Lawyers for the shoe scene fan club rest their case.

The Absent-Minded Professor (1961). In the first half of the basketball game the team was losing 46–3. Then Fred MacMurray makes the team wear his special sneakers, made of flubber, a material that gains energy every time it strikes a hard surface. This allows the players to jump to amazing heights and they win the game 47–46. Shoe scene aficionados have a special feeling for this loopy scene because it is the only time in movie history that shoes have affected the outcome of a high school basketball game.

Wall Street: Money Never Sleeps (2010). Shoe scene fans start tapping their feet in anticipation when they learn that Gordon Gekko has turned the $100 million he stole from his daughter into $1.3 billion. The first thing he does after he buys a bunch of suits is to go to the best shoe store in London. The shoes we see on the shelves probably start at $1,000 a pair. Gekko, while getting fitted by the salesperson, interrupts his cell phone conversation to look down and matter-of-factly tell the shoe clerk, "I'll take four of these." The fact that we never see the shoes Gekko is referring to is a stroke of Oliver Stone genius. It allows the membership to imagine the shoes in the window of Church's English Shoes that they have always longed for but could never afford to buy.

SHOPPING

Starting Over (1979). It's rare that a shopping scene gets a unanimous thumbs-up from fans of this genre but this one did. No shopping scene fan is able to resist when Burt Reynolds has an anxiety attack while shopping for a bedroom set in Bloomingdale's. When his brother (Charles Durning), a psychiatrist, shows up, he takes one look at Reynolds, who is hyperventilating, turns to the crowd and asks, "Anyone got a Valium?" Literally everyone does and Reynolds is saved in this very funny and sharp scene. It just goes to show that when a shopping scene is really good, nothing has to be bought.

Pretty Woman (1990). Nothing is bought by Julia Roberts when she walks into that shop on Rodeo Drive with a fistful of money. The problem is that the store doesn't serve women who are dressed like prostitutes ... and who actually are prostitutes. But Hector Elizondo saves the day when he sends Roberts to his personal shopper and she winds up looking so good that Richard Gere hardly recognizes her. The expressions on the faces of the two Rodeo Drive salesladies when Roberts pokes her head into their store and shows them all her packages is particularly satisfying to shopping scene aficionados.

The Big Lebowski (1996). Most people get dressed up to go shopping, but Jeff Bridges doesn't even get dressed. Shopping in his bathrobe and sunglasses for the half-and-half he needs to mix his white Russians, Bridges picks a carton from the shelf, sniffs it, then shows up at the checkout counter with drops of half-and-half in his beard. What won over the shopping scene crowd is that when he gets to the checkout counter, he writes the cashier a check for 69 cents.

Darling (1973). The food shopping scene in this movie had to be withdrawn from consideration because Julie Christie doesn't pay for all the gourmet food items she stuffs into her purse. Since there is currently no Best Shoplifting Scenes in the Movies Fan Club, sympathetic shopping scene fans who have a soft spot for shoplifting scenes were permitted to submit a recipe that includes as an ingredient Marsala wine, one of the items that Christie stole.

SHOPLIFTER'S ZABAGLIONE

Steal a bottle of Marsala wine and 6 eggs. You'll also need to steal 6 tablespoons of sugar. In a large bowl, beat six egg yolks and gradually add the sugar and two-thirds of a cup of wine while beating.

Place the mixture over boiling water and whip vigorously with a wire whisk that you stole until the custard foams up in the pan and begins to thicken. Run out and steal a small box of strawberries and add them to the mixture. Serve warm in stolen sherbet glasses. Serves four.

Author's Note: Do not use the can of prawn curry that Julie Christie stole.

SKIING

Downhill Racer (1969). There are two great skiing scenes in what many moviegoers consider to be the best skiing movie ever made. As Major Strasser says in *Casablanca* when Claude Rains tells him that he is about to arrest the man who killed the courier and stole the letters of transit, "I expected nothing less." The first scene is that long, leisurely shot of Robert Redford and Camilla Sparv skiing down the mountain after their love affair has begun. The music is pretty nice, too. The second is at the very end of the movie, when Redford skis the race of his life in the downhill to put him in the lead for an Olympic gold medal. The camera work is so realistic that you can even hear Redford's skis chattering as he flies down the mountain. What puts this scene over the top is that while Redford is being congratulated by the press, he looks up at the timing clock and sees that the skier making the next run is beating his time. Then, less than a hundred yards from the finish, the skier falls. The press goes back to crowding around, but Redford keeps looking at the fallen skier, a boy of barely eighteen, who looks back at Redford with an expression of heartbreaking disappointment on his face.

The Mortal Storm (1940). Margaret Sullivan never gets to finish her ski run to Austria with Jimmy Stewart. Trying to flee the Nazis, she is shot. She then asks Stewart to pick her up and carry her across the border so she can die in a free country. Interestingly, this is one of the few anti–Nazi movies released before America got in the war.

Spellbound (1945). Gregory Peck doesn't like the parallel marks Ingrid Bergman makes in the tablecloth with her fork. So she takes him skiing, and as they approach a cliff, Peck remembers that he didn't kill his brother. He also remembers his name. Nothing like a good ski run to clear the cobwebs. There was also a concerto written to accompany what many regard as the phoniest-looking ski scene ever shot, even though Bergman was coached by an Olympic skier to make it look real. After a few mugs of *glug* (an apres-ski cocktail that includes wine, brandy and rum), ski scene nuts will admit that it was only the shortage of realistic ski scenes in movies that landed this one on the list.

The Pink Panther (1963). At least David Niven knew how to ski, but few ski scene aficionados believe that the flying ski jump rescue of Claudia Cardinale was done by him. It really wasn't his movie anyway, as most of his scenes were stolen by Peter Sellers.

SLOW DANCING

Rain Man (1988). Of all the beautiful women Tom Cruise could have chosen to dance with, he chooses Dustin Hoffman. The scene in the hotel room where he teaches his autistic brother how to dance is a perennial favorite of the slow dancing fan club. Cruise is preparing Hoffman for his date with Iris, a hooker. He puts on some music and warns his brother that he has to touch someone when he dances. "I'm not gonna hurt you," he says. Then he tells Hoffman to watch his feet. But after a while he tells him he has to look up sometimes. He also tells Hoffman that he has to lead. Cruise is so moved that toward the end of the scene he tells Hoffman that he feels like giving him a hug. A great scene that is worthy of its inclusion. Hoffman is reported to have told friends that it was his role as Dorothy the nurse in *Tootsie* (1982) that made learning how to lead so difficult.

Picnic (1955). "You used to dance like that, Flo." That's what the elderly lady tells Kim Novak's mother (Betty Field) as they watch William Holden and Novak dancing to "Moonglow" at the Labor Day picnic. It's a line that captures the pleasures of slow dancing and one that continues to thrill slow dancing movie fans everywhere.

The Way We Were (1973). Slow dancing devotees know how James Woods feels when Robert Redford cuts in on him to dance with Barbra Streisand at the senior prom because Streisand would never look at him the way she looks at Redford as they dance. Maybe Streisand was simply wondering why Redford was still in college at the age of 37.

Slow dancing scenes that are admired but didn't make the cut include *They Shoot Horses, Don't They?* (1969), because the dancers looked too tired, and *Beauty and the Beast* (1991), because Rule #4 in the slow dancing charter states that waltzes cannot be considered for an award. Though Burt Lancaster's waltz with Claudia Cardinale in *The Leopard* (1963) was lovely, it was also not allowed for the same reason. Ditto for the Yul Brynner and Deborah Kerr waltz in *The King and I* (1956). Uma Thurman and John Travolta's slow dance in *Pulp Fiction* (1994) almost made it in, but in the end it did not, because they never touched each other while they danced. Coming closest to making the cut was Kenneth Branagh's slow dance with his monster creation (Helena Bonham Carter) in *Frankenstein* (1994).

SPIDER

Annie Hall (1977). When Diane Keaton calls Woody Allen up in the middle of the night and asks him to come over to kill the spider in her bathtub, spider scene fans know they are in for a treat. Allen doesn't let them down. Yes, he asks for a can of Raid first, admittedly a poor start, but he redeems himself by doing the job with a tennis racket. He nearly achieves spider scene perfection by popping out of the bathroom every few seconds to inform Keaton of his progress and telling her that it is not one spider he is dealing with but two.

Arnold Zellermeyer, in his capacity as D.O.A. recording secretary, was present at the vote. He has this note to add: When one of the members wanted to discuss how it must have felt to be Shelley Duvall, the actress Allen left behind when he went over to Keaton's apartment, she was stripped of her membership and her subscription to *Spider Scene Quarterly* was cancelled on the spot.

Dr. No (1963). Though it is true that the 007 designation gives James Bond the license to kill spiders, many film fans have asked themselves whether 19 blows with a shoe wasn't somewhat excessive. That is one of the questions spider scene fans had to deal with before deciding whether this scene would be consigned to oblivion or marked for film history. The fact that Sean Connery, who plays Bond, was sick in the bathroom after the spider squashing is reported to have had some effect on the voting.

To be fair, some spider scene fans felt this was a normal reaction to a tarantula crawling up his body while he slept. Unfortunately, this argument only led to another question: "Why was the spider covered up by a sheet through so much of the scene?" Lawyers among the tarantula scene subcommittee of organized spider scene fans are surprisingly reluctant to reveal their true feelings about this scene, citing simply *ipso facto*, meaning its presence in this book speaks for itself.

The Thief of Bagdad (1940). A favorite entertainment at spider scene fan club get-togethers is to ask first-time guests what was the first line of the song Sabu sings when he climbs the giant spiderweb. It's a good question, one that no true spider scene fan would ever fail to answer. The line, of course, is this: "I want to be a sailor, sailing out to sea." Some film fans may regard this type of amusement as unusual, but then spider scene fans have always been considered a bit strange. A lot of this may have to do with their inability to resolve their love-hate relationship with spiders. They hate spiders but they love film scenes with spiders. These dual feelings are best illustrated in the choice of this scene. Spider scene fans admit the giant spider gets less frightening with each viewing but voted for it because Sabu kills it. It has been said that psychiatrists, upon discovering that they have a spider scene fan as a client, often have a difficult time restraining themselves from shouting "Yippee!" during the session.

The Fly (1958). So accustomed are spider scene fans to seeing spiders get killed, they no longer shush David Hedison when he is crying, "Help me," after he gets caught in the spider's web. Nor do spider scene fans blame themselves when the spider (and Hedison) are crushed by the policeman in the final scene. To be completely accurate, it is not quite all of Hedison that is caught in the web — just his head and one of his arms.

Spider scene fans love spider scenes so much they can be excused for overlooking the fact that the web and the spider in this film look as if they are more likely to be seen in a rain forest than in a private home. It is a powerful scene nevertheless and keeps intact their record of never rewarding a spider scene in which a spider doesn't get killed.

The Incredible Shrinking Man (1957). Another spider bites the dust in this original (and best) version of the film when Grant Williams stabs it with a sewing needle. The argument between Williams and the spider was over a crumb of bread. The spider needed it in order to live and keep growing. Williams needed it in order to live and keep shrinking. Since there obviously wasn't enough food in the cellar for both a spider and a shrinking man, there was no objection raised by the authorities when it was discovered that the spider was killed with an unregistered sewing needle.

Dracula (1931). It somehow seems fitting that the one spider to survive a spider scene lives in Castle Dracula. Bela Lugosi puts it eloquently when he observes, "The spider spinning its web for the unwitting fly. The blood is delight." Spider scene fans still wonder how Lugosi got through the spiderweb without breaking it. Renfield, who was following only a few steps behind, practically had to chop his way through it. Spider scene fans see only two possible answers to this question, which has puzzled them for more than eight decades: either vampires can walk through spiderwebs without breaking them or the spiders in Castle Dracula are unusually nimble when it comes to spinning webs.

STEAMBATH

T-Men (1947). Nearly every afternoon at 2:17 P.M. a member of the steambath scene fan club, carrying a bag of Chinese litchi nuts, walks into the steamroom. A minute later, two other members lock him in and turn up the steam. The member inside bangs on the door, puts his face up to the glass window and shouts for them to let him out. At this point all the members of the club who are present gather in the steamroom area and chant, "Schemer, Schemer, Schemer," before they let him out.

This ritual is in honor of Wallace Ford, the actor who played "Schemer," the character in this film who was murdered by being steamed to death in his favorite steamroom. Many steambath fans consider it to be the greatest steambath scene ever filmed. Steambath scene fans now believe they have pinpointed the precise time of day "Schemer" was murdered and like to re-create the crime each afternoon when there is a quorum present at the club.

Eastern Promises (2007). Thanks to director David Cronenberg, steambath violence has come a long way. The brutal scene in which two Russian Mafia hitmen walk into a steamroom and attack a naked Viggo Mortensen with knives is so hard to watch that some steambath scene aficionados admit to voting it in without being able to watch the scene through to its grisly knife-in-the-eye climax.

Spartacus (1960). Steambath scene fans have long been accused of turning to ancient Rome whenever they need a good steambath scene and this choice is often cited as proof of the validity of that accusation. This is vigorously denied by steambath scene legalists, who point out that the steambath scene between Charles Laughton and Laurence Olivier stands on its own. When one considers what might have happened if Laughton hadn't informed Olivier that he had made a deal with the Silesian pirates not to take Kirk Douglas and his slave army to Greece, steambath scene fans might be right. The slave revolt would have succeeded, Douglas would have lived past the end of the film and more Greeks would have had clefts in their chins.

Gorky Park (1983). One might not think that steambath scene fans are particularly sensitive to beauty, but they are. Many consider the Moscow (Helsinki, actually) steamroom in this movie to be among the most beautiful they have ever seen. A balcony surrounds a huge pool. There are private rooms where one can rest after a steam. Tables of caviar and blini are set up everywhere so members can eat well while they replace the body's need for salt. So beautiful is the place that when a sliver of food escapes onto William Hurt's upper lip, it so mars the splendor of this steamroom that Lee Marvin feels compelled to make Hurt aware of it with the words, "Man overboard."

House of Strangers (1949). The steambath scene in this rarely shown Joseph L. Mankiewicz gem is often used by steambath scene fans to illustrate the restorative powers of steambaths for a wide range of problems. Richard Conte goes there because he's having trouble with his girlfriend, Susan Hayward. His father, Edward G. Robinson, is worried about the authorities looking over "the books." So what's their solution to these problems? More steam.

STUTTERING

The investigation took two years and it was only a lucky break that brought the first real lead. Had the investigative reporter on the case not been a Jimmy Stewart fan, he would never have spotted the five men leaving a movie theater at the beginning of *The Man Who Shot Liberty Valance* (1962). The group left right after a minor character was trying to order his meal. There was no doubt. The scene they had come to see was definitely a stuttering scene. All the guy could get out was "Dee-Dee-Dee..." So the impatient waitress trying to get him to finish says, "Deep-dish apple pie?" and he says, "Yeah."

As the group walked out, one of them was heard to say, "I'll b-bet th-that probably wasn't what he wanted." Following them back to a house on 92nd Street, the reporter realized that he had found the headquarters of the reclusive stuttering scene fan club. Denied entrance, the reporter tried posing as a Chinese delivery man. But all he could find out was that stutterers are good tippers. The only information that round-the-clock surveillance added was that the stuttering scene fan club's weekly poker game was held on a Thursday. Months went by. It was only after the theatrical release of the movie that made stutterers famous that stuttering scene aficionados dropped their reclusive ways and gave the world's movie nuts what they wanted: their list of the best stuttering scenes in film history. It is re-created on these pages.

The King's Speech (2010). Colin Firth did for stutterers what Mikail Baryshnikov did for ballet dancers — he made it okay to be one. He also corrected the assumption that the only time stutterers don't stutter is when they sing. Thanks to Firth we now know that stutterers also don't stutter when they curse. The scene that stuttering scene fans enjoy the most is when Lionel, the king's eccentric Australian speech therapist (Geoffrey Rush), prods Bertie (Colin Firth) to lose his cool, forcing him to sing out a symphony of shit-fuck-bugger-me swearing (all stammer-free). The scene is quite effective because earlier we had seen Firth, then merely Prince Albert, trying to speak at the British Empire Exhibition. The words stuck in his throat, and his silences between syllables filled the stadium. It's why Firth comes to Rush when he becomes king, telling Rush that the nation believes that "when I speak, I speak for them. But I can't speak." When Firth finally gives the speech for which the film is named, stuttering scene fans are relieved to see Rush standing like a conductor in front of the king, helping him get through it without a single stutter. It is not surprising that the film's writer, David

Seidler, was a stutterer himself, or that he won an Academy Award for his screenplay and didn't stutter once during his acceptance speech.

The Right Stuff (1983). The real-life stuttering problem of astronaut John Glenn's Annie kept Vice President Lyndon Johnson waiting outside her house after Glenn's space flight. To stuttering scene movie nuts, it was Glenn (Ed Harris) who showed the right stuff when he backed up his wife and told her she didn't have to talk to anyone she didn't want to.

My Cousin Vinny (1992). There's only one reason a stutterer would ever want to become a trial lawyer: to give stuttering scene fans a great stuttering scene. Austin Pendleton's opening speech in the courtroom, where he can hardly get a word out, has made him, rather than the loudmouth lawyer Joe Pesci, the hero of stuttering scene fans everywhere.

A Fish Called Wanda (1988). Because Kevin Kline is so mean to Michael Palin when he stutters, this film is the only movie in film history to cause an uproar among stutterers. The charge is that the film depicts stutters as pushovers Members of the stutterering scene fan club, however, value the film. They point out that the nervous and awkward Palin, who is constantly and sadistically bullied by Kline, shows how difficult and painful stuttering can be.

There is a special corner in the stuttering scene clubhouse where framed photographs are hung, showing stutterers who are killed or tortured in the movies they are in. Prominently shown are photographs of Terance Stamp, hung for stuttering in *Billy Budd*, (1962); Brad Dourif, who committed suicide in *One Flew Over the Cuckoo's Nest* (1975); and the captured partisan in *Pan's Labyrinth* (2006) who was promised that he would be let go if he could count to three without stuttering.

It is not generally known, but a movie scene that always strikes fear into the hearts of the club members occurs in *What Ever Happened to Baby Jane?* (1962). It is the moment when Victor Buono asks his mother to make a phone call for him so he can apply for the pianist's job advertised by Joan Crawford and Bette Davis. Buono is not a stutterer, nor is stuttering even hinted at in the entire film. What strikes such a responsive chord among stutterers in the club is that they themselves often do the same thing as Buono because, to a stutterer, speaking on the telephone is terrifying and always something to be avoided.

As Porky Pig would say, "Th-th-that's all folks!"

SUICIDE

It is a statistic studied by suicide scene fans everywhere: in the United States alone more than 30,000 people die each year from suicide. Among the elderly, falls from high places and gun shots are most popular. Hanging is the most common form of suicide among young men. Which is why the clubhouse has no ceiling beams and is on the first floor of a three-story brownstone. Members must also pass through a metal detector to get inside. A secret ballot of favorite suicide scenes in film showed the following results:

Humoresque (1946). Referred to by suicide cognoscenti the longest suicide scene in film history is Joan Crawford's final goodbye to John Garfield.

Humoresque (1946). Considered to be the longest suicide scene in film history is Joan Crawford's farewell to John Garfield.

First she drinks a whole decanter of whiskey while she is listening to Garfield playing Wagner's "Liebestod" on the radio. Then, finally, she goes out onto the terrace and stumbles down to the beach. We still hear the music as she walks along the water's edge. Crawford passes a man and his dog. There is a nice long shot of waves crashing. Then an underwater shot. The man with the dog looks back. The beach is empty. There is just a close-up shot of a crumpled flyer with Garfield's photograph. A four star suicide scene if there ever was one.

The Shawshank Redemption (1994). This film was placed first in the voting because it has not one, but two suicide scenes. James Whitmore is the first to go. Whitmore has been in prison for 50 years and can't handle it when he is released. Inside he's an important man (the prison librarian) but outside he can't even get a library card. A few weeks after his release he hangs himself from a ceiling beam at the halfway house where he has been living. But as sad as Whitmore's suicide is, the prison warden's (Bob Gunton) suicide never fails to get a cheer. About to be arrested for stealing money from the state, the rat who refused to review new evidence that would have freed Tim Robbins blows his brains out.

Rules of Attraction (2002). The suicide in this film almost equals Joan Crawford's in screen time but it's a lot more disturbing. Not only do few suicide scene fans like this movie, but fewer still can bear to watch when the unnamed college student slashes her wrists in the bathtub. Her reason? She's heartbroken that the boy she wanted to make love to at the "Dressed to Get Screwed" party left with another girl. What makes the scene even more heartbreaking is the Harry Nilsson song, "Without You," played on the soundtrack while she is dying. Great song. Lousy movie.

Jules and Jim (1962). A much lighter suicide scene occurs in this delightful Francois Truffaut film. Technically, when Jeanne Moreau drives Jim (Henri Serre) over that broken bridge, it is what the police call a murder/suicide. But not even this surprise ending can dim the charms of the early relationship between Moreau, Serre and Oscar Werner. Suicide scene fans, more than anyone else, know that only the French can make suicide so captivating.

Thelma and Louise (1991). Director Ridley Scott must be a big fan of *Jules and Jim* because he pulls the same kind of surprise ending. Even though the only man in the film who is anywhere near decent is Detective Hal Slocum (Harvey Keitel), most men in the suicide fan club still feel sorry for Thelma (Geena Davis) and Louise (Susan Sarandon) when they drive off that cliff.

Death in Venice (1971). Though most movie fans think that Aschenbach (Dirk Bogarde) died of cholera in this under-appreciated Luchino Visconti film, members of this fan club know for a fact that it was suicide. Bogarde knew the city of Venice was gripped by a cholera epidemic, but if he couldn't have Tadzio (Bjorn Andresen), life wasn't worth living. So he stays to get that one last glimpse of Tadzio on the beach and dies with the mascara running down his cheeks to the beautiful strains of the Adagietto from Gustav Mahler's Fifth Symphony.

Meet John Doe (1941). Suicide scene fans must have a soft spot for Gary Cooper. Okay, he doesn't jump off the roof of City Hall on Christmas Eve like he said he would. But every filmgoer knows that he really meant to jump, and would have if Barbara Stanwyck hadn't rushed up there and talked him out of it. Besides, if anyone should have jumped, it should have been her. She wrote the damn suicide note in the first place.

The Front (1976). A little-known fact, but one well known to suicide scene fans, is that actors who are about to commit suicide overtip. That's what blacklisted comic Hecky Brown (Zero Mostel) does after he checks into a hotel room on a high floor. He orders up a bottle of whiskey, overtips the waiter, drinks half the bottle, and jumps out of the window. However, the movie audience doesn't see Mostel jump; the camera simply shoots the open window. Mostel was no stranger to the blacklist, having been on it himself in the 1950s. But he didn't name names.

In Bruges (2008). A special dispensation allowed the attempted suicide of novice hitman Colin Farrell to be considered in this category. He would have gone through with it had not Brendan Gleeson, who was about to shoot him, prevented Farrell from doing so. It's scenes like this that give suicide movie nuts a good feeling about themselves.

In an extraordinary session, the actor Bud Cort was banned from joining the suicide scene fan club because of all those faked drownings and faked hangings he pulled on his mother (Vivian Pickles) in the 1971 dark comedy *Harold and Maude*.

SWEARING

Four Weddings and a Funeral (1994). Even the most hardened fan of profanity in movies found it hard to believe there would ever be a scene where a charmer like Hugh Grant would ever say the f-word. But he does. It's the opening scene of this lovely film when Grant wakes up late and is rushing to attend wedding #1, where he is the best man. He utters the f-word seven times. The members of the club always count them. Should there be doubters, here they are: "Fuck ... fuck ... fuck. I'm late. Fuck ... fuck ... fuck ... fuck!'

My Cousin Vinny (1992). Swearing scene fans know not to ask Marisa Tomei what to wear when they go hunting. Here's what she would say: "Imagine you're a deer. You're prancing along. You get thirsty. You spot a little brook. You put your little deer lips down to the cool, clear water — BAM. A fuckin' bullet rips off part of your head. Your brains are lying on the ground in little bloody pieces. NowI ask ya, would you give a fuck what kind of pants the son-of-a-bitch who shot you was wearing?"

Glengarry Glen Ross (1992). Alec Baldwin knows how to give a motivational speech to the salesmen in a Chicago real estate office: "First prize is a Cadillac El Dorado, second prize is a set of steak knives, third prize is you're fired!" But first Baldwin has the grace to introduce himself: "My name is 'fuck you'!"

Pulp Fiction (1994). The scene in which Tim Roth and Amanda Plummer hold up the diner ranks pretty high with cursing scene fans. Plummer stands up, gun in hand, and screams, "If any of you fucking pricks move, I'll execute every motherfucking last one of you!"

Planes, Trains, and Automobiles (1987) Steve Martin knows his way around the f-word when the rental car he reserved isn't where it's supposed to be, "Well, I don't appreciate the way your fucking company gave me fucking keys to a fucking car that doesn't fucking exist. And I really don't appreciate having to walk across a highway and across a fucking runway to have you smile in my fucking face." That the car rental person is a lady is a masterly touch.

Had it not been for a surprise police raid, there would have been 43 more swearing scenes. Happily, in a plea bargain deal, members of the swearing scene fan club were released the next morning in their own recognizance. There was one stipulation: the members had to watch 100 hours of singing cowboy movies. At the 12-hour mark the members knew that Champion was the name of Gene Autry's horse and that Roy Rogers rode Trigger. A tiny majority of the singing cowboy fan club (formerly the swearing scene fan club) thought Gene Autry was a better actor than Roy Rogers but the majority was so small as to be statistically insignificant. The sidekick vote was much clearer. Sixty-three percent of the recently released swearing scene fan club thought Smiley Burnette was funnier than Gabby Hayes. The vote on this may have been influenced by the fact that Burnette rode a horse like a real cowboy and could play five instruments at the same time. Hayes didn't learn to ride a horse until he was in his forties. But what weighed heavily in Gabby's favor with some members of the now-defunct swearing scene fan club was that every once in a while he would let out with a "dad-bust-it!"

SWIMMING POOL

Sunset Boulevard (1950). It has been called the greatest pool scene that Hollywood ever made. Had the movie not opened with the body of William Holden floating face down in Norma Desmond's (Gloria Swanson) swimming pool, this film could not have been made. That's because Holden was able to tell the story of how he got into this predicament even though he had already been shot by Swanson. Regrettably, swimming pool scene fans can't leave after this scene unless they want to pay another admission charge because the movie ends with Holden back in the pool.

The Graduate (1967). For pool scene fans, it is, as Dustin Hoffman's father (William Daniels) says, "a feat of daring in water that is over six feet deep." That is the signal for Hoffman to walk out of the house in diving gear (complete with breathing sound effects) and enter the pool, A nice birthday present, sure. But it is much more. The underwater shot in the pool of Hoffman standing there in his diving gear is the perfect way to depict the uncertainty felt by most college students after they graduate. As Barbra Streisand said in *The Way We Were* (1973), "Commencement is a pretty strange word for 'the end.'"

William Holden would gladly have settled for a slap in the face from Gloria Swanson if he knew what was in store for him in the swimming pool at the end of *Sunset Boulevard* (1950).

Harold and Maude (1971). The scene in which Harold's mother (Vivian Pickles) walks to the swimming pool and dramatically disrobes to the strains of Tchaikovsky's Piano Concerto No. 1 and then goes in and swims to the other end, passing Harold (Bud Cort) who is lying face down while fully clothed, without even a side glance, is priceless. Cort has pulled this kind of stunt before, but the Best Hanging Scenes Fan Club claimed first dibs and wouldn't allow pool scene fans to describe it.

True Lies (1994). It's not Arnold Schwarzenegger who gets the applause from swimming pool scene fans, but Art Malik, the terrorist who jumps his motorcycle from the roof of a Marriott Hotel into a pool 10 stories below. When Schwarzenegger tries this stunt, the stolen police horse he is riding chickens out and Schwarzenegger is left dangling over the edge. Since both

Malik (on his motorcycle) and Schwarzenegger (on his horse) rode up to the top floor of the hotel in an elevator, elevator scene fans raised the roof. But the matter was settled when the D.O.A. pointed out that they had already voted the previous scene as one of their top elevator scenes and could not use it again. That settled the matter and the scene remained in the Best Swimming Pool Scene in Movie History category.

Goodbye Columbus (1969). This near-perfect adaptation of the Philip Roth novella also contains a pretty good pool scene. You can tell this film is set in the 1950s because while Richard Benjamin is lying in a lounge chair by the pool, there's a cha-cha playing on the loudspeaker. That pool scene movie nuts also have a romantic side is demonstrated by the fact that they know that when Ali McGraw hands Benjamin her sunglasses to hold before she dives into the pool, in the very next scene Benjamin will phone her for a date, identifying himself as the guy who held her sunglasses.

It's a Wonderful Life (1946). "Did you know there's a swimming pool under this floor? And did you know that button behind you causes this floor to open up? And did you further know that George Bailey is dancing right over that crack?"

So begins the iconic scene where Jimmy Stewart and Donna Reed fall into the swimming pool while trying to win the Charleston contest. Swimming pool scene researchers have discovered that the swimming pool used in this scene is located in the Beverly Hills High School and is still in operation. They also found out that director Frank Capra agreed to pay a bonus of $25 to any teen willing to jump into the pool on cue during the scene's memorable climax.

TANGO

Scent of a Woman (1992). The orchestra at the Waldorf starts playing a tango. A blind colonel (Al Pacino) picks up the scent of a beautiful young woman seated two tables away. He asks the young prep school student who is taking care of him over Thanksgiving weekend for the dimensions of the dance floor. Pacino then approaches her table and asks the young woman to dance with him. She protests that she doesn't know how to tango. Pacino charms her onto the dance floor. The rest is tango scene history.

True Lies (1994). This movie never would have gotten made if it weren't for Arnold Schwarzenegger's tango coach. When he told her he was afraid of making a mistake, she looked him in the eyes and told him, "There are no mistakes in the tango." Schwarzenegger felt so good afterwards that he repeated the tango he did with Tia Carrera at the beginning of the film with his wife, Jamie Lee Curtis, at the end of the movie. Schwarzenegger's tango (complete with a rose in Curtis's mouth) is so nice to watch that Tom Arnold couldn't resist complaining about always having to be in the surveillance truck.

The Tango Lesson (1997). The tango is a great cure for writer's block. Filmmaker Sally Potter becomes obsessed with the tango and offers dancer Pablo Verón a part in her movie in exchange for tango lessons. The result is a tango scene on the smoky stage of a theater that takes the audience's breath away. The film, shot in black and white, is a favorite of tango fans who don't like technicolor.

Strictly Ballroom (1992). The stylized, over-the-top tango of ballroom dancing almost gives tango scenes a bad name until Paul Mercurio adds a few maverick touches of his own. A lovely film from Australia.

Assassination Tango (2002)/*Shall We Dance?* (2003). In a side bet, the tango scene fan club voted Robert Duvall a better tango dancer than Richard Gere, even though Gere had Jennifer Lopez as a partner. The membership also thought the 1996 Japanese film (*Shall We Dansu?*) was a lot better.

The Four Horsemen of the Apocalypse (1921). At the end of every meeting the tango movie nuts who are still around play the tango scene that made Rudolph Valentino a superstar. He's a lot better than Gere and Duvall, a little better than Schwarzenegger but not nearly as good as Pablo Verón. What fascinates the membership is that during Valentino's dramatic tango, a drunk watching him sees a goldfish in his beer.

TELEPHONE

Owning a cell phone is grounds for expulsion from the Telephone Scene fan club. That's why the article in the *New York Times* about a movie chain in Texas that throws out anyone in the audience who is talking or texting on a cell phone received so much applause from the club. It also gave the voting for best telephone scene in movie history more meaning as well as a dash of subtext. It was a marathon session and the results contained a surprise.

The Birds (1963). In this Hitchcock film portraying bird anger at not being able to use the public telephone it's no surprise that Tippi Hedren takes shelter in a phone booth.

But anyone who has made a long phone call from one knows what happens next. Squawking sea gulls fly around the booth and one particularly impatient gull butts his head against the glass cracking it. Interestingly, bird scene fans and telephone scene fans have agreed to disagree on where this scene should be placed. Bird scene fans do not think birds are yet capable of dialing a phone and that Tippi Hedren must have irritated the birds in another way. Telephone scene fans think the birds got mad because Hedren was in that phone booth too long and that birds, like people, have every right to bang on the glass of a public telephone booth when they have an important call to make.

To back up their argument, they cite the moment when an impatient guy, his face all bloody, tries to get in but Tippi won't let him. From the booth Tippi is able to see the entire bird attack. To heighten the tension, Hitchcock shoots her from above as she's moving around the phone booth in a panic.

Dial M for Murder (1954). The English have a lot more phone booth patience than seagulls. Ray Milland shows admirable restraint at his club when the gentleman on the phone has a long conversation that prevents Milland from dialing his home to signal the murderer behind the curtain. To the relief of phone booth scene fans Milland gets through in time. But the gentleman he hired to murder Grace Kelly isn't so lucky. Kelly stabs him with her sewing scissors. The scissors didn't go in his back too deeply, but the dumb schmuck followed Alfred Hitchcock's directions and fell on his back, plunging the scissors in all the way.

Recently discovered notes found in the telephone scene clubhouse revealed that many members were dismayed when they found themselves watching a movie about someone trying to murder Grace Kelly. At the same time, they were flattered that their favorite instrument was being used to set up the murder and were able to judge the scene with a fair degree of equanimity. The scene does have a surprisingly high tension level. First, Ray Milland's watch stops so the call that will bring Kelly to the phone to be strangled is late. Then there is the strangler impatiently waiting behind the drape for the call that will bring Kelly to the telephone. Finally, there is the strangling attempt itself (which Milland can hear over his phone) and Milland's surprise and disappointment at finally reaching Kelly and finding her alive. Telephone scene fans agree that while the film itself has become somewhat dated, the telephone scene holds up surprisingly well.

Goodfellas (1990). The big surprise in the voting is that pay phone scene movie nuts would even vote for a scene where a pay phone is treated so badly. When Robert De Niro hears the news that his pal and partner in crime, Joe Pesci, was murdered, he's so grief stricken and angry that he bangs the phone until it's smashed and knocks the phone booth over.

Dirty Harry (1971). Any movie fan who has ever passed by a ringing pay phone and was tempted to pick it up has pretty good precedent. It's why Clint Eastwood rushes all over San Francisco to pick up ringing pay phones. He's trying to prevent the murder of a young girl and the serial killer is giving him clues every time he reaches a ringing phone.

Get Smart (2008). Would you believe that a phone booth can be used as an elevator to travel underground? Maxwell Smart does. He uses a telephone booth to get to HQ. Harry Potter used a London pay phone to reach the Ministry of Magic, but did not make the cut because the pay phone fan club by laws only allow one movie pay phone elevator to be chosen.

I Know Where I'm Going (1945). Michael Powell and Emeric Pressburger know how to make lovely movies, but they certainly don't know a lot about pay phones. The pay phone in this charming film is placed in the middle of nowhere, right besides as raging waterfall. Pay phone scene fans love it however, even though it is nearly impossible for anyone in the booth to hear the other party.

Network (1976). Though best known for its window scene ("I'm mad as hell and I'm not going to take it anymore!"), this Sidney Lumet film also contains a nasty telephone scene that must rank as one of the all-time great date-breaking moments in screen history. It occurs at the beginning of the William Holden–Faye Dunaway affair. Holden has just asked Dunaway if she's doing anything that night. Her response is to pick up the telephone, dial a number, and say to whomever it was who answered, "I can't make it tonight, darling. Call you tomorrow." She then hangs up before she gets a response. Telephone scene fans were so affected by Dunaway's glacial phone manner that they once began to draw up a list of people she may have broken the date with. Some of the names on that list were quite surprising.

Force of Evil (1948). Pound for pound, John Garfield may have been the best telephone scene actor in the business. Revered by telephone scene enthusiasts, he had a special way of expressing fear over the telephone that no actor could duplicate — he licked his lips. The great lip wetting scene in this film is set up by Marie Windsor when she tells Garfield that his phone may be tapped. "If you listen carefully, and try it several times, you can hear a little click," she tells him. Windsor, who has a thing for Garfield in the movie, rubs it in when she reminds him that he might spend the rest of his life trying to remember what he said over that phone.

Later, alone in his office, Garfield picks up the phone to see if it really is tapped. Telephone scene fans in the audience are usually at the edges of their seats as Garfield runs his tongue over his lips while holding the phone to his ear. When the "click" is heard, Garfield's eyes grow visibly wider, another nice touch. But Garfield hasn't exhausted his bag of telephone tricks yet. After he hears the "click," he dials the time. When the time lady tells it to him, Garfield actually starts doing it again, running his tongue over his lips. Telephone scene fans are still debating this one. Was Garfield showing off or did he really think the telephone time lady was tapping his phone?

Mildred Pierce (1945). Veda (Ann Blyth) would have known Joan Crawford would never tell the police on her if she had paid more attention to this award-winning scene, which telephone scene fans like to think of as representing "telephone mother love at its height." When Crawford picks up the phone after Blyth shoots Zachary Scott, even occasional telephone fans know she isn't going to turn her daughter in. They know it from the look Crawford gets on her face when the spoiled Blyth tells her, "It's your fault as well as mine."

If one catches a telephone scene fan at a particularly indiscreet moment, they will admit to knowing a lot of actresses who would have turned Blyth in, especially after finding out that Bylth and Scott had been fooling around in secret. But not Crawford. No, this is mother love's shining telephone moment and Crawford plays it for all it's worth, winning the votes and admiration of telephone scene fans everywhere.

Like stuttering scene fans, telephone scene fans have a particular soft spot for Victor Buono, who in *What Ever Happened to Baby Jane?* couldn't get up the courage to make the call that would get him a job as Bette Davis's accompanist. So he does what any red-blooded American pianist would do: he asks his mother to make the call for him.

Another actor who attracted the notice of telephone scene fans is Chevy Chase. In *Funny Farm* (1988), every time Chase tries to dial a number on his newly installed phone, the operator asks him to deposit 20 cents. The problem is that there is no place to put the coins because the phone is not a pay phone. In an inspired attempt to get his call through, Chase drops two pennies in a glass jar. It doesn't fool the operator, but it does mark him as a telephone scene actor to watch.

TRAIN

Dollars (1972). A lucky moment for Warren Beatty and a very satisfying one for train scene fans is when Scott Brady drinks a champagne bottle full of undiluted LSD. Brady doesn't like it much, though, and has a fit, made all the more horrifying because it takes place in the close quarters of a train compartment. Whatever was in that bottle, it was Brady's realistic thrashing and twitching that won this scene its laurels.

Strangers on a Train (1951). It's a good thing that shoe scene fans, train scene fans and train station scene fans are so friendly or the decision about which category the key scene in this film should be placed in might still be in dispute. The problem lies in the opening sequence of scenes, which starts in a train station but ends up on a train. The camera first picks up a pair of flashy black-and-white men's shoes. It then cuts to an ordinary pair of men's shoes. Both pairs of shoes seem to be rushing to catch a train, but at no time is the audience allowed to see above the knee.

The four shoes board the train and sit down at the same table. Both pairs of shoes cross their legs and the shoes unintentionally brush one another. The shoes, of course, belong to two of the most popular train scene heroes in recent screen history — Robert Walker and Farley Granger. It is on this train, while having lunch in his compartment, that Walker makes his now-famous proposal to Granger: "You do my murder. I do yours."

Of more than marginal interest is the fact that Walker's idea for two strangers to switch murders comes just after his idea of making a reservation on the first rocketship to the moon. Officials at NASA were not displeased when Walker did not make it through the film alive. Had he, they might have had a murderer taking mankind's first step on the moon.

A welcome bonus, and one that train station scene fans graciously allowed to be mentioned in this category, is the sight of Alfred Hitchcock, the film's director, boarding the train carrying a bass fiddle.

The Lady Vanishes (1938). Proof that Alfred Hitchcock knew his way around a good train scene is the one in a dining car where Dame May Witty writes her name (FROY) with her finger on the fogged-up train window for Margaret Lockwood. When Miss Froy disappears from the train, no one believes she existed and Lockwood is beginning to believe she imagined the entire episode until the train goes through a tunnel and the letters F-R-O-Y reappear on the window. Pure Hitchcock and pretty wonderful at that.

Shadow of a Doubt (1943). There's something about Hitchcock and great train scenes. In this film, Joseph Cotten, Teresa Wright's favorite uncle, tries to throw her off a moving train because she has figured out he's the Merry Widow serial killer. But in the struggle he falls into the path of a moving train.

Murder on the Orient Express (1974). Most train scene fans were surprised that it was Sidney Lumet, not train scene maven Alfred Hitchcock, who directed this film. But Lumet comes through, getting even with Richard Widmark for pushing the old lady down the stairs in *Kiss of Death* (1947) by having him stabbed to death by 12 of the passengers. Ingrid Bergman won an Academy Award for Best Supporting Actress for her role as a missionary in Africa on the strength of one line: "I vant to help little brown babies who are less fortunate than myself."

Slumdog Millionaire (2008). It is a train window once more that catches the attention of train scene movie nuts. The two young boys who ride on the roof of a train only descend to sell the passengers trinkets. Club members' favorite scene in this lovely film is when the smaller of the two, held by his feet by his older brother, descends from the train roof to steal pancakes through an open window from diners in a first-class carriage.

Butch Cassidy and the Sundance Kid (1969). Train scene buffs don't normally like to see trains get blown up, but they admit that when trains get destroyed in the kind of lighthearted way Paul Newman and Robert Redford do things, it takes the sting out. Poor Woodcock, though. The railroad clerk put in charge of the money has put a steel safe in the railroad car. Newman isn't sure if he used enough dynamite and winds up blowing the freight car to smithereens. The money goes flying all over the place and armed deputies on horseback burst out of a freight car in a second train that has been following the first.

Once Upon a Time in the West (1969). Jason Robards is a big favorite of train scene fans if only for his remarkable skill at hanging from a moving train by his feet and still being able to shoot someone in the head through a train window. The scene is set up marvelously. First, we hear Robards's footsteps on the train roof. A gunman follows the footsteps from inside the train. Charles Bronson, tied up in a chair, adds a lot to the excitement with some pretty neat reaction shots. The footsteps stop. There is a tapping on the train window. The gunman turns. Robards's face appears in the train window. Robards smiles at the gunman. Bronson smiles at Robards. Robards aims his gun and shoots the gunman in the head. All in all, a nifty little train scene in a surprisingly good spaghetti western that's played to the hilt by all concerned.

A Hard Day's Night (1964). This highly eccentric train scene was nearly kept off the ballot because the movie in which it appeared was thought to be a music video. What made it look like a music video was when the Beatles, told not to play their radio by the stuffy Englishman seated in their compartment, are next seen running (and bicycling) beside the train while asking if they can have their ball back.

One avid supporter of this particular scene pointed out that any scene which has a stuffy Englishman saying to the Beatles, "I fought in the war for your sort," and Ringo responding with the words, "I'll bet you're sorry you won, then," had to be a real movie. When his line of reasoning did not impress the voting panel, the only three train scene fans old enough to see the film when it originally came out stepped forward and testified that the film did indeed play in movie theaters. It was this evidence that finally cleared the way for this scene to be listed on the ballot, saving it from movie scene oblivion.

TRAIN STATION

The Dresser (1984). Train station scene fans have always been leery of ham actors when they go near a train station. Their fear is justified by Albert Finney, who, as the actor-manager of a traveling theatrical group, points his walking stick at the departing train he was rushing to catch and shouts in his deepest, most dramatic voice, "Stop ... that ... train!" In a screech of brakes and a cloud of smoke, the train stops. Train station parapsychologists have so far been unable to explain Finney's unusual effect on trains except to say they will soon be publishing a monograph titled *If You Can Intimidate Trains, the World Is Your Oyster.*

Brief Encounter (1945). Not many film fans are aware of it, but the main sitting room of the train station scene fan club is an exact reproduction of the train station tea shop where Celia Johnson and Trevor Howard carried on most of their extramarital affair. Before entering this room, a visitor is required to bathe their left eye in a glass of water, just as Celia Johnson did when she got that cinder in her eye. This ritual, of course, re-creates the scene in which Johnson meets Howard, the doctor who removes the cinder and falls in love with her.

Train station scene fans are still amazed at how Johnson managed to bathe her eye with an ordinary glass of water without spilling one drop on her dress. One theory is that it was not an ordinary glass, but an eye cup that was kept in the tea shop especially for passengers who were prone to cinders. This opens up the possibility of other train station affairs beginning in the same way, affairs that Noel Coward chose not to write about. But all that is another kettle of tea. Regardless, the movie is enormously popular with train station fans worldwide. Their favorite line in the film? When Celia Johnson, concerned that Trevor Howard will miss his train, says to him, "Don't bother about me. My train's not due for two minutes."

In the Heat of the Night (1967). When Rod Steiger, who plays a small-town sheriff, says to Sidney Poitier, who plays a big-city detective, "Virgil, you take care, you hear," in the last scene of the film, we know why train station scene fans suspended the "100-foot rule" and voted this scene its just award. Steiger's words are so full of unspoken feeling and Poitier's farewell smile so full of tenderness that the fact that the railroad station measured less than the required 100 feet (as is stated in the train station scene fan club by-laws) was quietly overlooked.

Summertime (1955). Scratch a train station scene fan and you'll often find a romantic. When Rossano Brazzi runs along the station platform after Katharine Hepburn's train while carrying that box of white gladiolas, they are all rooting for him. So, Brazzi didn't quite manage to catch the train, but he does open the box to show her that they are white gladiolas. These are the same flowers she lost in the canal. When Hepburn sees them, she at least knows that he loves her. Train station fans not so romantically inclined point out that if this weren't Venice, Brazzi would have been in better shape (one can't jog each morning on the Grand Canal) and might have caught up with Hepburn's train. Then he could have given her the flowers and she could have taken them back with her to the States.

Love in the Afternoon (1957). In Venice, it's the men who unsuccessfully bring flowers to women at train stations that (such as Rossano Brazzi in *Summertime*); in Paris, it is reversed and the women bring flowers to the men. Yes, the flowers Audrey Hepburn is seen holding are for Gary Cooper, but she never gives them to him. To get them, Cooper has to swoop Hepburn onto the train and take her back to America with him. Train station scene fans have always wondered what would have happened had Brazzi been lucky enough to get within Katharine Hepburn's swooping range.

Mr. Hulot's Holiday (1953). The very funny train station scene at the beginning of this film would have won its award without being asterisked had train station scene fans not invoked their exclusivity rule. It states that no train station scene can be given an award if other scenes in the film have already received one. Since this Tati film already had both a cemetery and a funny walk scene award when the voting took place, it could only be relegated to this sidenote. The scene in question, of course, is charming — one in which a group of tourists, listening to the announcement of what track their train will leave from, is continually made to shuffle from one platform to the next. Naturally, when the train finally arrives, they are on the wrong platform.

UMBRELLA

Foreign Correspondent (1940). The only scene in this movie that interests umbrella scene fans occurs at the very beginning when an assassin is trying to escape from Joel McCrea through a throng of umbrella-toting bystanders. Alfred Hitchcock shoots the scene from above and the audience never sees McCrea or the assassin. All they see of the chase are rippling umbrellas. The assassin is never caught but by then the umbrella scene fans have left the theater and repaired to the bar.

The Umbrellas of Cherbourg (1964). Only the beauty of Catherine Deneuve got this sappy film a mention. The only time we see umbrellas is during the opening credits, when Deneuve is looking through her widowed mother's umbrella shop at her lover. That the umbrellas during the opening credits are shot from above is a nice homage to Hitchcock, but it wasn't enough for a vocal minority of umbrella scene fans to table their motion to strike this movie from the list.

Singin' in the Rain (1952). Now here's an umbrella scene that umbrella scene fans can sink their galoshes into. Their only complaint is that Gene Kelly doesn't know how to hold an umbrella. After he kisses Debbie Reynolds goodnight, he holds it an angle, and then when he starts dancing he folds it up. According to umbrella scene aficionados, this is a sure sign a guy's in love. There's also a lot of nice puddle splashing and a lamp post to hug. At least Kelly's wearing a hat. And at the end of the scene he gives his umbrella to a passerby who opens it up and uses it the right way. The movie is now 60 years old and that scene still holds up.

Mary Poppins (1964). After 31 viewings of Mary Poppins arriving from that cloud over London, the umbrella scene fan club have determined the secret of Julie Andrew's ability to use her umbrella like a parachute. They have observed that she keeps her feet in the ballet "first position"—heels together but feet spread as far as they will go. They also noted that the nanny who quit to make room for Andrews also had an umbrella. Some even recognized her as the ever delightful Elsa Lanchester. An interesting side effect of being able to use an umbrella to fly through the air is that you will be able to slide not only down but also up a bannister. That, in a word, is supercalifragillisticexpialidocious.

The Private Life of Sherlock Holmes (1970). A mild disappointment to Sherlock Holmes fans, but a delight to umbrella scene fans, is that this Billy Wilder film contains a truly amazing umbrella scene. What's more, it is the only time an umbrella has been used to send Morse code. At the very end of the film, when Genevieve Page is leaving in the coach, she signals goodbye to Holmes with her umbrella, using Morse code to spell out "a-u-f—w-i-e-d-e-r-s-e-h-e-n."

Black Narcissus (1947). When those raindrops begin to fall in the final scene of this film, umbrella scene fans all offer their umbrellas to David Farrar. He hasn't got one, you see. Farrar had given Deborah Kerr and the other sisters until the rainy season to fail and pack up for home and he was right. Farrar watches Kerr head down the trail as the rain gets heavier. You can see it hitting his eyelashes. The nuns start putting up umbrellas but Farrar has none. But what can you expect from a man who kicked the beautiful Kathleen Byron out of his house when she offered herself to him? Okay, she was crazy, and she was a nun, but still....

VAMPIRE

Love at First Bite (1979). Though Dracula's (George Hamilton) dance with Susan Saint James is pretty nifty, the vampire scene fan club preferred Richard Benjamin flashing a Star of David at Hamilton and being told by Hamilton that he should go find himself a nice Jewish girl. But when it came to the final vote, the scene vampire movie nuts liked most was the one where Dracula is being thrown out of his castle in Transylvania. One guy in the crowd is particularly angry because Dracula bit his mother. Hamilton stops and asks the man his name. When the man obliges, Dracula replies, "I not only bit your mother, I bit your grandmother, too."

Dracula (1931). When vampire scene fans are offered a glass of wine, their response is always the same. In their best Bela Lugosi accents they say, "I don't drink ... *wine.*" The scene that vampire fans cherish most in this early film about their favorite undead fiend is when Renfield leans out of the coach taking him to Dracula's castle to tell the driver (a disguised Dracula) to slow down and he sees that the driver has disappeared, and a bat is leading the horses.

Love at First Bite (1979). You have to be a 700-year-old vampire (George Hamilton) to be able to say, "I not only bit your mother, I bit your grandmother too" (Susan Saint James, left).

Interview with the Vampire (1994). "I'm flesh and blood. But not human. I haven't been human for 200 years." That's how Brad Pitt explains it when he tells Christian Slater the story of his life. Bela Lugosi may have his charms but you have to admit that Pitt is a much more beautiful vampire than he is. Ditto for Tom Cruise. It is interesting that the scene which has vampire scene fans drooling is when the child vampire (a young Kirsten Dunst) gets her first taste of blood and says, "I want some more."

The Twilight Saga (2008–2012). After sitting through the entire *Twilight* series, an elderly vampire aficionado was heard to remark, "You mean there are teenagers who aren't vampires?" When word of this spread to the members, it resulted in the Bela Lugosi Agreement. The agreement states that no film from the I vampire saga could ever be considered for an award. Old Bela would definitely approve.

From Cinema Paradiso: In a rare extra edition of Arnold Zellermeyer's newsletter, it was announced that the vampire scene fan club, which only uses its clubhouse after sundown, has agreed to share its space with fans of bank robbery scenes, who only meet during banking hours.

VIAGRA

You Will Meet a Tall Dark Stranger (2010). Viagra fans — better make that Viagra movie scene fans — don't have a lot of movies to choose from but what they have is choice stuff. When Anthony Hopkins marries the gold-digging hooker (Lucy Punch) after dumping his wife of 40 years (Gemma Jones), even the most militant feminist begins to feel sorry for the guy. The scene where Punch wants to get it on and Hopkins has to pop a pill and plead with her to wait three more minutes is heart-stirring.

Scary Movie 4 (2006). The world may be attacked by aliens, but for Viagra scene movie nuts, the only scene worth watching is when Charlie Sheen pops a bottleful of Viagra and gets a boner so big the cat thinks it's a scratching post. Sheen's leap over the balcony and his landing on his concrete-breaking erection has the membership rushing to the pharmacist to get their prescriptions refilled every time.

Two Weeks in Another Town (1962). Though scientists remind us that Viagra wasn't available to the public until 1998, Viagra movie scene nuts firmly believe you could get it in Italy in the early 1960s during the shooting of this film. They cite the scene in which an Italian movie mogul tells Kirk Douglas over lunch that on resuming his weekly visit to a prostitute, his 90-year-old father held up two fingers instead of the usual one to let his son know he had done it twice.

Encouraged by the D.O.A's willingness to give this scene a place in its Viagra scene collection, members of the Viagra scene fan club (average age 73) offered the D.O.A. its recipe for Logan's Swiss Steak. It was accepted unanimously.

LOGAN'S SWISS STEAK
(*Logan's Run*, 1976)

This is the meal you should make yourself when the button in your palm starts to blink and you are about to get zapped by a disintegrator ray because you have reached the age of 30.

INGREDIENTS
6 boneless chuck steaks
6 carrots, peeled and sliced
1 large onion, quartered
1 can of peeled tomatoes
3 stalks of celery, diced
1 bay leaf
salt
pepper
flour
½ cup of red wine

Dredge the steaks in flour to which salt and pepper has been added. In a skillet, brown the steaks well and toss them into a large pot. Add the carrots, tomatoes, onion, celery and bay leaf. Pour in the wine and cook everything on a low flame for about three hours. Serve with mashed potatoes. Very comforting.

WHIRLPOOL

I Know Where I'm Going (1945). There's no way around it. Once you mention a whirlpool in a movie, there has to be a small boat that gets caught in one. The whirlpool in this Michael Powell — Emeric Pressberger gem is "Corryvrecken," the third largest whirlpool in the world. When Roger Livesey and Wendy Hiller's boat's engine becomes flooded, they are caught in it. It is a fearsome whirlpool indeed, but Livesey is able to restart the motor just in time and they escape. The cast includes the strangely beautiful actress Pamela Brown, who has long been forgiven by whirlpool scene fans for treating Kirk Douglas so badly in *Lust for Life* (1966).

Moby Dick (1956). One of the neatest ways to get invited to a whirlpool party is to be waved in by a dead, peg-legged sea captain who's lashed to a white whale. Gregory Peck, as Ahab, does his part. Moby Dick takes over when he head butts the *Pequod* to smithereens, then swims around it at high speed. The whirlpool he creates sinks the ship. To a whirlpool aficionado, this is the best possible way to end a movie.

About Schmidt (2002). A roar of protest from the whirlpool scene fan club was caused by the D.O.A.'s decision to allow whirlpool baths into the whirlpool scene category. For years the governing body was between Scylla and Charibdis on this matter. Their long-awaited decision had a lot to do with a naked and seductive Kathy Bates slipping into the hot tub and placing her hand on Jack Nicholson's knee underwater. It was the expression on Nicholson's face that won them over.

WHISPERING

Lost in Translation (2003). At a special news conference the whispering scene fan club announced that they had learned what Bill Murray was whispering to Scarlett Johansson in the final scene of this movie. Murray was telling Johansson that she's lucky she already graduated from Yale because in a few years college tuition would start to rise dramatically. Sofia Coppola, who wrote the screenplay, did not go to Yale, but wanted to keep her options open in case any members of the Academy were Ivy Leaguers. And that's why she kept what Murray was saying inaudible. Coppola simply didn't want to put Ivy League colleges in a bad light.

White Heat (1949). Prison scene fans nearly rioted when the D.O.A. allowed Jimmy Cagney's crackup in the prison mess hall to also be counted as a whispering scene. The ruling was based on the amount of time Cagney spent crawling on the mess table and punching prison guards (14.2 seconds) compared to the amount of time it took for Cagney's question ("How's my mom doing?") to reach the prisoner at the other end of the mess table and the amount of time it took for the answer (She's dead") to be whispered back to Cagney (14.3 seconds).

Key Largo (1948). Whatever Edward G. Robinson whispered to Lauren Bacall that caused her to slap him in the face had to be suppressed until the words "blow job" could be used in polite society.

Both *The Blair Witch Project* (1999) and *The Haunting* (1963) were ruled ineligible and ran for bragging rights only. For a whispering scene to be valid, both the whisperer and the whisperee must be seen on the screen.

WHISTLING

To Have and Have Not (1944). It was Rule 6 that finally cleared the way for this whistling cult favorite. Rule 6 in the *Whistling Scene Manual* (revised edition) states; "A whistling scene need not contain an actual whistle if either an oral or written description of a whistle is given." Any whistling scene fan worth his or her wind could be woken up in the middle of the night, hung by his or her toes and still be able to recite Lauren Bacall's unforgettable exit line to Humphrey Bogart: "You know how to whistle, don't you? You just put your lips together and blow."

The High and the Mighty (1954). Ever since the first viewing of that unforgettable final scene when John Wayne walks away from the plane after having kept it from crash-landing into the ocean, the whistled tune played on the soundtrack has had an effect on film fans that has lasted long after the movie ends. Whistling scene fans report that throughout the year the film was released, they would hear that tune whistled by motorists running out of gas, by spouses returning home without a birthday present, and even by passersby on the way to the dentist.

They argue, and rightly so, that no whistling scene that has become such a widespread symbol for courage in the face of adversity should ever be denied its place in film history. If this wasn't reason enough for its selection, whistling scene fans point out this was the movie that gave Robert Stack the courage he needed to try out for his role in *Airplane* (1980).

The Bridge on the River Kwai (1957). What inspired Alec Guinness's regiment to begin whistling the "Colonel Bogie March" as they marched into that Japanese POW camp is still being pondered by whistling scene fans. Nevertheless, the effect is quite remarkable. So good were they that when the men appeared to be whistled out, a full marching band joined them on the soundtrack. Even Sessue Hayakawa, the camp commander, was impressed.

David Lean, the director of this film about the positive effects of whistling on POWs, thought it was so good that he made it the opening scene. John Hughes, director of *The Breakfast Club* (1985), liked it so much he borrowed it for his film about troubled teenagers. In Hughes's whistling scene, one of the boys in detention class starts whistling the same "Colonel Bogie March." The other teenagers join him until they are all whistling it. Then a band on the soundtrack joins in, until marching music fills the classroom. Though it is certainly a whistling scene of award caliber (that the teens are sitting down while whistling a march is an especially nice touch), it couldn't be considered for a whistling scene award. Whistling scene rules clearly state, "When a whistling scene is duplicated in another film, it is the whistling scene in the earlier film that shall be deemed eligible for the award." Since *The Bridge on the River Kwai* was made nearly 30 years before *The Breakfast Club*, the later film can be nothing more than an interesting whistling sidelight.

Snow White and the Seven Dwarfs (1937). Whistling scene fans as a group are certainly not afraid to take risks. They include not one but two animated features on their list. In the first, which also happened to be Walt Disney's first full-length feature production, the whistling is done at work to a song most movie fans still remember—"Whistle While You Work." This selection, however, was the cause of some disharmony among male and female members of the judging panel. The dwarfs (Dopey, Grumpy, Sleepy, Sneezy, Doc, Happy, and Bashful) whistle while they work in their diamond mine. Snow White whistles while she cleans up their cottage. The matter was resolved when it was agreed that the film was made at a time when male and female roles were less overlapping.

Pinocchio (1940). In this second animated feature to be listed, whistling scene fans like to point out the importance of whistling scenes in teaching a moral lesson. When Jiminy Cricket starts to sing, "Take the straight and narrow path, and if you start to slide, give a little whistle, and always let your conscience be your guide," whistling fans take this message to heart. You can usually spot whistling scene fans in the audience. Whenever Pinocchio starts doing dumb things, they are whistling. It's something Pinocchio should have been doing when he met Stromboli. If he had, he never would have grown those donkey ears.

M (1931). Whistling scene paparazzi still insist that Peter Lorre whistled in this Fritz Lang classic because he was nervous about it being his first film. This notion was quashed once and for all by whistling scene historians, who report that the whistling was definitely in the script. The only way the blind balloon vendor could discover the identity of the child murderer was to recognize the tune Lorre whistled when he bought balloons for the children he planned to kill.

An interesting footnote is that the tune Lorre was originally supposed to have whistled was from Strauss's *Tales from the Vienna Woods*. Unfortunately, soon after the film began shooting, it was discovered that the only tune the blind balloon vendor could recognize was the first few bars of, "In the Hall of the Mountain King" from Grieg's *Peer Gynt*. Lorre was not so familiar with this tune, which explains why so much of his whistling is off key.

It should also be noted that balloon scene enthusiasts have had a longstanding claim to this scene. However, it was judged that since the whistling element was more important to the film than the balloon element, the scene should be placed in the whistling category. Since whistling scene fans do not allow their scenes to be considered for other category awards, here it remains.

The King and I (1956). Deborah Kerr surprised whistling scene fans with a pretty snappy rendition of "Whistle a Happy Tune," to ease her son's fears about meeting the King of Siam. (Whistling as a cure for apprehension has always counted a lot with whistling scene fans.) By the time Kerr begins to sing to her son about the benefits of whistling and her son begins to feel better about meeting Yul Brynner, whistling scene fans were completely won over. That her voice was dubbed by Marni Nixon was never concealed by Kerr and had no effect on the voting since her whistle was real.

Among the many actors who made the most of their whistling scenes, two stand out: Leslie Howard, whistling "Oh, there's a tavern in the town" as he steps into the fog and across the Swiss border in *Pimpernel Smith* (1941), and Christopher Plummer, who as Captain Von Trapp in *The Sound of Music* (1965) made up for his lack of whistling ability by using a bosun's whistle to call his children.

WINDOW

Chariots of Fire (1981). No window scene has ever generated as much emotion as the one in which Ian Holm looks out of his Paris hotel window and sees the British flag being raised above the Olympic stadium to the strains of "God Save the Queen." To Holm, who played Ben Cross's track coach, it meant that Cross had won the race and the gold medal. Holm, an actor who certainly knows how to look out of a window, was so overcome by emotion that he had to sit down. Window scene fans feel that because this shot was framed through the narrow confines of a hotel window, the emotional impact of the scene was greatly heightened.

In an effort to publicize what a good window scene can do for a movie, window scene fans have sent clips of this scene to producers and directors of every movie-making nation. The results of this public relations effort are not yet conclusive.

The Bad and the Beautiful (1952). One of the strangest window scenes ever to come out of Hollywood takes place in a car. When Lana Turner discovers that Kirk Douglas doesn't love her anymore, she rushes out of his mansion and drives off in her car. When Turner sees drops on the window, she turns on the window wipers. But it isn't raining and they are not raindrops. She's crying and what she thought were raindrops were really tears. Back when this film was made, this was considered a pretty nifty scene. Today, it seems rather silly (but not to window scene fans).

Rear Window (1954). Though seasoned window scene fans certainly appreciate the multiplicity of window scenes that Jimmy Stewart is privy to in this movie—Judith Evelyn (Miss Lonely Hearts) having dinner with her imaginary suitor; the dog being lowered down to the courtyard each day; the dog's murder; the beautiful but fickle dancer and her suitors; the sensitive composer; the newlyweds; and, of course, Raymond Burr, his complaining wife and the suspicious goings-on in that apartment—it is the marvelous sequence of denouements to these window vignettes that they find most pleasing. Miss Lonely Hearts finally meets the composer, the dead dog's owners get a new dog, the fickle dancer's runty boyfriend returns from the army, the honeymoon couple start bickering, Burr gets caught, Stewart breaks his other leg falling out of the window, and, most important of all, Burr's old apartment becomes vacant. In a city where good apartments are so hard to find, that is something worth murdering for.

Beverly Hills Cop (1984). There are only two possible window shots. In window scene jargon they are called "innies" and "outies." An "innie" is when the camera is inside and looking out. An "outie" is when the camera is outside looking in. On rare occasions, a window scene comes along that is both an "innie" and an "outie." It usually causes quite a stir among fans of this genre, as it did when Eddie Murphy got thrown out of that plate-glass window in Beverly Hills. The camera was outside looking in and Murphy was inside being thrown out. When Murphy got arrested for being thrown out of the window, it became rarer still: a window scene that is also quite funny.

The Day of the Jackal (1973). A window scene that is both funny and frightening occurs near the end of this Frederick Forsythe adaptation about a plot to assassinate Charles de Gaulle. Crouching at a window overlooking the Tomb of the Unknown Soldier, Edward Fox has de Gaulle in the sights of his homemade rifle. The French general has just stopped in front of a very short dignitary. At the instant Fox fires, de Gaulle bends down to shake the near midget's hand. As a result of this politeness, the bullet flies harmlessly over his head. Had the dignitary he was shaking hands with been anywhere near normal height, de Gaulle would have been successfully assassinated.

Raising Arizona (1987). A very funny window scene—quite unique, in fact—was inserted into this sometimes funny movie about a couple who kidnap a baby quintuplet. It's shot from the baby's POV (which is screenwriter talk for "point of view") and somehow it works. The baby is facing the window and looking at Nicolas Cage, who is on a ladder looking in. Because the baby is being bounced by his nanny, the camera bounces, too. The result of all this is that we see Cage moving up and down as he would be seen by the baby he is about to kidnap. Window scene fans love this kind of stuff and gave it their highest rating.

Network (1976). The bimonthly meetings of the window scene fan club are always open and I happened to attend the one in which this satire on window use was selected. Though the winning scene's luster has been slightly diminished by time, window scene fans are still thrilled when they see windows all across the nation opening and people popping their heads out and yelling, "I'm mad as hell and I'm not going to take it anymore!"

This is the first time such an orchestrated chorus of window yells have ever appeared on screen and it certainly deserved its award.

Epilogue

The annual Christmas party of the Devotees of Film Art, held this year in Los Angeles, was a huge success. The party was held at the original Barney's Beanery in West Hollywood. With 85 different beers to choose from, along with 45 chile dishes, it has become a magnet for movie nuts. More than 500 members, including wives and significant others, attended. Louis Blank, the newly sworn-in president, opened the proceedings on a light note. He told the members how easy it was for native Californians to tell he was just visiting because he the only one in this town who ordered a single-dip cone at the local Baskin Robbins; everyone else ordered a double-dip. Blank then got down to business, awarding the Movie Nut of the Year statuette to Bruno Arbuthnot. Arbuthnot won the coveted award for helping the model airplane scene fan club produce their own model airplane movie. The 31-minute film, loosely based on *Spirit of St. Louis*, involved Bruno's attempt to be the first person to fly from Montauk, Long Island, to New York City in a rubber-band-powered model airplane. Bruno, an experienced pilot, believed that by braiding the rubber band, it would last the entire flight. He was wrong, and Bruno was forced to land in Babylon, Long Island, 39 minutes of flying time short of New York City. Bruno ended his acceptance speech by thanking his mother for keeping him home from school on rainy days when he was in first grade so they could watch Joan Crawford movies at the Loew's Paradise. He also thanked Hardy Kruger, one of the stars of *Flight of the Phoenix*, for giving him the idea.

Afterwards, everyone headed for the open bar to reminisce about their own formative years and the hours spent they had spent watching *Million Dollar Movie* and *Picture for a Sunday Afternoon*. Movie nuts particularly remembered atmospheric films like *Mask of Dimitrios* (1944), *The Paradine Case (1947)*, *Cat People* (1942), *La Strada* (1954), *Shadow of a Doubt* (1943) and *Lost Horizon* (1937). Few could understand how Louis Jourdan could let Joan Fontaine go in Max Ophul's *Letter from an Unknown Woman* (1948). Favorite actors often mentioned included George Sanders for his role in *The Private Affairs of Bel Ami* (1947) and Hurd Hatfield and Angela Lansbury for their roles in *The Picture of Dorian Gray* (1945). After a few drinks, Arnold

Zellermeyer stood on the bar and performed "Goodbye Little Yellowbird," the song Lansbury sang in that film. Someone did a pretty good imitation of John Garfield listening to check if his phone had been tapped in *Force of Evil* (1948), wetting his lips and widening to perfection. This was Garfield at his peak. At 4 A.M. when the bar closed, I slipped a DVD of *The Mask of Dimitrios* into one of the television sets. No one left.

The End*

Not the 1978 movie with Burt Reynolds and Dom DeLuise.

Index